John Pendleton Farrow

The Romantic Story of David Robertson

John Pendleton Farrow

The Romantic Story of David Robertson

ISBN/EAN: 9783744708852

Printed in Europe, USA, Canada, Australia, Japan

Cover: Foto ©Thomas Meinert / pixelio.de

More available books at **www.hansebooks.com**

THE ROMANTIC STORY

OF

DAVID ROBERTSON,

AMONG THE ISLANDS, OFF AND ON THE

COAST OF MAINE.

BY

CAPT. JOHN PENDLETON FARROW.

ISLESBORO, MAINE.

BELFAST, MAINE:

PRESS OF BELFAST AGE PUBLISHING COMPANY,

1898.

PREFACE.

The following interesting story, strongly protrays the life and customs among the hardy sailors and fishermen, who fiftv years ago were to be found along our entire New England coast. It is written in that dialect, and with phrases then common with those hardy followers of the sea. The story was written by Capt. John P. Farrow of Islesboro, who for many years has lived and followed the ocean with these people, whose deeds of daring and heroism have done so much to enrich American history. Capt. Farrow was born in Islesboro, and received a liberal education at Belfast, Maine, and at Cambridge, Mass. At an early age he began following the ocean, and being a great student of human nature and possessed of a retentive memory he retired after a long and honorable career on the ocean, with a well stored mind of incidents and reminiscences, which he put into manuscript form, and at the solicitation of his friends he consented to place this book before the public. In writing this book he has drawn but little from imagination, as all of the principal actors were people who were known personally to the author. In placing this book before the public it is confidently believed that the reader will find much of historical interest and value and preserve a history of a people who were once a distinctive class, but who today are fast conforming to modern forms and ways, by a closer contact with a busy world which is fast encroaching upon their hitherto secluded homes.   F. I. W.

CHAPTER I

REMINISCENCES and history of David Robertson who spent more than twenty years on an island situated on the eastern coast of Maine, occupying his time in summer in his fishing boat with his gun and dog, being upwards of seventy years of age before he received his orders from the Great Commander for his watch below.

David was born near one of the tributary streams of the Kennebec River in Maine, in the year 1815. His father came of the Puritan stock and was a strong advocate for the purity of his religion. He did not believe in sparing the rod and spoiling the child. David came in for more than his share of the rod in his own estimation. David seemed or appeared to "take out of kin," making very little talk and being quiet and reserved in manners, while his noisy brothers generally managed to have the blame laid on David when things went wrong.

His mother would sometimes advocate David's cause, but generally let Mr. Robertson correct the children as he thought best, her time being occupied with looking after the small children, one for every other year of her married life, with the last one or baby in her arms shoving his little fist in her hair trying to see how much he could pull out.

One day David saw Mrs. Brown's geese in his father's grain field. He threw a stone at them and unexpectedly killed one of the geese. He immediately went to Mrs. Brown and offered to do anything that he could for her to pay the damage, saying to her he was very sorry. Mrs. Brown said to him, " Never mind, say nothing about it." Sometime after, his father hearing about it gave David a whipping because he had not told him. David in reply said, " There must be some place better than home for me," brooding over his wrongs that were real or imaginary, the whole winter.

What few days he could go to school—he studied hard and excelled in mathematics and geography, with his mind made up that it would be his last winter at home. Things went from bad to worse and his father gave him more of the drudgery to do than was his share "to take the sulks out of him " he said.

He did not understand David when all he wanted was a kind word or some encourage-ment; then how willingly he would have done his duty, but the blue laws of those days must be obeyed, viz. spare the rod and spoil the child.

This winter of 1828 was the mildest ever known. Mr. Robertson was employed at cut-ting logs to haul to the saw mill to make boards and shingles to build a framed house to take the place of the log house built by his father.

David now being thirteen years old was large enough to do the teaming, with two yoke of oxen, to the mill five miles away, making two trips a day. His father could not spare him from the team to go to school, as Mr. Robertson's means were limited with his large family.

Everything they ate besides barley bread and potatoes with milk, was considered a luxury. Mr. Robertson gave his son David no praise, but was quick to censure him if anything went wrong.

David being sensitive and doing more thinking than talking, became moody and peevish, his disposition soured which lasted him to a certain extent all through his life, but a kinder boy or man the sun never shone on. Here can be applied the old maxim with truth, " Just as the twig is bent the tree's inclined."

The spring was early and labor hard and unremitting was the lot of Mr. Robertson and his family, while Mrs. Robertson had to cook, wash, spin, weave and take care of her dairy. If she had had time to think, it would have discouraged a saint, but born of hardy New England stock, she went about her work with a cheerful animated countenance, and when a neighbor would drop in for a few minutes' chat, her pleasant face beamed with happiness and her tongue run nineteen to a dozen.

On winter evenings, the family sitting around the old fireplace, with half a cord of wood piled on the fire dogs, seemed to enjoy life, notwithstanding the hardships they had to endure. Such was the home David was about to leave, and in after years the old kitchen would come vividly to his mind when sitting in his cabin, and the scene was never forgotten by him as long as he lived.

In the early spring, no busier place could

be found than the Robertson homestead getting ready to build the new house, and on
no account must the farm work be neglected.
So up and at it early and late were Mr. Robertson and his boys. Inheriting the vigorous
constitution of their Scotch, Irish and English
ancestors, they were capable of enduring privations and hardships of the severest kind; but
the hard work and meager fare was at last too
much even for David's inherited constitution.

One afternoon when plowing in the field he
said to his father, " I am sick and want to go
home and tomorrow I will be able to finish
the plowing." His father replied, "David,
you are sulky and want to shirk your work,"
but reluctantly told him to put the team up
and go home. Next day David was taken
down with a fever.

This was the last work he ever did on the
old home farm. The scenes enacted here are
only a repetition of many similar scenes on

the old New England farms. Is it any wonder that their sons want to leave their rural
and paternal homes and look for greener
pastures in other lands? David's fever had a
run of twenty-one days. He had no doctor
to give him drugs and bleed his life away.

With his strong constitution and good nursing and nourishment, he soon became conva-
lescent. His father had seen but little of
him during his sickness, but when he found
that he was improving fast, he said to him,
"Your sickness has put us back with our
spring work and I expect you to help us as
soon as you are able." David replied, "Father,
I shall never help you any more. I shall go
away tomorrow." His father was dumb-
founded to hear this from David who had
never given him a word back in his life.

Next morning when the day star arose,
David, with a bundle containing a shirt and a
pair of stockings, with two Spanish milled

dollars in his pocket, the tears running down his cheeks, started and walked away.

When it was known that David was gone, Mrs. Robertson went into hysterics. Mr. Robertson sat gloomy, dismal and melancholy, and the once happy home of the Robertsons was broken.

CHAPTER II

SKIPPER Davis was a short, thick-set man past sixty years of age, once a sailor now a fisherman. His dress when on shore was a short, blue jacket with white pearl buttons, a blue shirt with a wide collar, a black silk handkerchief tied in a square knot, and if he had a waistcoat, no one ever saw him wearing it. His trousers were big enough in the legs to hold the shanks or legs of a man that was twice the size of Skipper Davis. On his head he wore a tarpaulin hat, his shoes or pumps as he called them, were ornamented with silver buckles, his hair once black was now gray and hung in curls on his shoulders, and he had rings in his ears representing foul anchors. One leg being two inches shorter than the other gave him a list to port, and his rolling gait made him conspicuous. He was a jolly, merry and hail fellow well met, and well known from Saccarappa to Quoddy Head. His boat was known in those days as a Chec-bacco boat, deriving its name from the place where it was built. His crew, to use Skipper Davis' own words "when he called the watch, out come one people." His man by the name of Jackson, he had picked up somewhere years before, and abbreviated his name to Jack. How old he was or where he came from was never known. If Jack ever had known, he had forgotten it.

In the township of Bristol near the shore of Muscongus Sound was situated the cottage of Skipper Davis. His wife, who was hale and hearty, although more than sixty years of age, was known as Aunt Nancy. A more motherly or kinder old lady was not to be found. "Her price is far above rubies, she openeth her mouth with wisdom," administer-

ing comfort in the time of trouble to all the
neighborhood, loved and respected by the old
and young.

Davis lived a neighbor to Commodore Sam-
uel Tucker, who moved from Boston to Bristol
in 1793, and died there March 10th, 1833.
Skipper Davis and Aunt Nancy were frequent
visitors to the Commodore's house, where they
always received a royal welcome. The Commodore was held in great veneration by Skipper Davis, who would swear for him, fight
for him and die for him if necessary.

The Skipper was with the Commodore in
the Increase at the time he captured the
privateer. Crown of Halifax, April 26th,
1813, and this was honor enough for him.
He was never tired of telling the story while
he lived, and all his intimate acquaintances
knew the story as well as he did.

Another story the skipper frequently used to
tell was about the Commodore, representing

himself as one of the principal actors of the scene. He had told it so often that he believed it himself, whether it was true or not. The Skipper said, "We had trouble with the proprietors regarding the running of the boundary lines and determined to have our rights if we had to fight for them. We called a meeting to see what we could do in regard to the matter. The meeting was in front of the school house, where a farmer's empty two wheeled cart was used for the speakers. After several had spoken, loud calls for Tucker were heard from all sides. I helped the Commodore to mount the cart, when up went the tongue and out we went, head, neck and heels a-hoy. The Commodore's speech was " I'll be d——d," when an uproar of laughter broke up the meeting."

Skipper Davis' besetting sin was his love for Medford rum, and once in a while it would get the better of him, causing his nose to have a vermillion hue, showing a tendency to bud and blossom. When under the influence of the beverage to a moderate extent, the effect it produced on him was to make him clever, well disposed, kind and honest; but taken in large doses and often, it gave him plenty of courage without sense. Such was the man that David served his time with for two years as a fishing lad.

When the sun rose David was miles away on his way down river. The beautiful spring morning revived him, the road was new to him and the scene was enchanting with now and then a glimpse of the river. Hope told flattering tales, but his mind would revert to the old log house, and he almost wished himself back. He could not help the tears coming to his eyes. A diversity of scenery greeted him while plodding his way down the river road and to a certain extent diverted his mind from his old home. On either side of the road grew stately pines which were sylvan and rustic. Nature was seen here in all her simplicity and beauty.

The sun was about two hours high when David came to a clearing, showing a farm house. He saw a woman going to the well and went to her assistance, carrying the pails of water to the house, and said to her, " I would like to do the chores for a bowl of bread and milk." She not only got him the bread and milk but the best she had cooked besides. The benevolence and attention to strangers in the humble cottages of the New England settlers are without precedent in the world.

David offered his services to the good housewife in return for what he considered his sumptuous fare. His appetite was good, having so lately recovered from the fever. It was really an enjoyment for this good woman to stuff David, but womanlike she could not help being inquisitive and trying to find out who David was and where he was going.

There was no ingratitude in David, and when she began to ask him questions, he hung his head and looked so sorrowful that her sympathy got the better of her inquisitiveness. David in his homely way thanked her, his looks expressing his gratitude. He then picked up his bundle and once more began his tramp down the river road.

After walking a mile or more, he thought his bundle seemed heavier and looked larger, and on investigation, he found a barley loaf with a piece of cheese of liberal size. How well such women are described by Solomon, viz: " She stretcheth out her hands to the poor and needy."

David continued on his way until the sun was past the meridian. Here the road assumed a different aspect, the primal forest trees having been cut down. When an abrupt turn in the road opened to his view the river town, he regarded it with admiration and some surprise.

He continued on a mile or more before arriving at the town. The scene was fascinating and for a time bewildered him. There were several vessels building, some of them of large size which particularly attracted his attention. Looking at them with wonder and surprise, not gazing or staring at them with impudence but with amazement, he finally went down to the wharf where Skipper Davis' Checbacco's boat lay. The man Jack was at work taking in freight alone.

The boat was five or six feet below the wharf where it necessitated Jack's getting from the boat to the wharf every time he hoisted a bag or box on board. Skipper Davis was up town with his cronies drinking Medford rum, entertaining the company with anecdotes of Commodore Tucker, leaving

Jack to get the freight on board as best he could.

David, looking on and ever willing to lend a helping hand, asked Jack if he should not help him. Jack was only too willing to have help, so David took hold with a will and stayed on the wharf to sling the bags and bales while Jack hoisted them on board with the throat halyards. David slung the first bag with a horse knot, which brought some criticism from Jack, but a better knot to sling a bag with has not been found since Noah took his cruise in the Ark. When the freight was all on board, and David had helped Jack stow it away in the hold and clear up decks, Jack said, "Now we will go below and get supper."

The boat cuddy was large, it being a fisherman with accommodations for six men. There was a brick fireplace with the chimney extending to the deck. The residue above

the deck was boards. David built a fire while
Jack stirred up an Indian Johnny cake, put it
in a Dutch oven and clapped on the iron cover,
then buried it in the ashes and coals. He then
put on the potatoes in a baking kettle and
hung them on the crane, frying the pork in
the skillet, made the tea, and the supper was
complete. The table was hung with leather
hinges, and it folded up against the foremast,
where it was out of the way when not in use.
When supper was ready Jack went after the
Skipper, leaving David to keep ship. When
Jack found the Skipper, he was mellow, tending towards intoxication, but would at once
have resented being told that he was drunk.
He would never acknowledge that he was
ever in that situation. His pumps were rights
and lefts, and by some mishap he had got
them on the wrong feet, which he never
would have done if he had not been hot,
(an expression invariably used in those days

for inebriety.) Jack got him aboard and down in the cuddy when the heat overcame him. Jack with the help of David got him into his berth, where he passed the night in oblivion, muttering something about the Commodore which was unintelligible.

An epicure wholly given to luxury could not have enjoyed a supper more than did David this meagre fare. Extremes met in the character of Jack and David, Jack doing all the talking, David the thinking. The evening spent in the cuddy was congenial to both. It was late that night when they turned in. The berths were hard, but David had hardly laid his head on the apology for a pillow before he was sound asleep.

CHAPTER III

EARLY the following morning the wind was to the northward blowing down river when Skipper Davis turned out, calling Jack. When Jack went on deck, he was followed by David and explained to the Skipper where David came from, and that he wanted to go with them. Skipper Davis questioned David whose simple, plain statement and artless manner at once enlisted the Skipper in his favor. David was shipped without due form for a cruise in the Checbacco boat, Skipper Davis commanding. No fisherman's stores for a cruise would have been complete without a liberal supply of Medford or its equivalent of West India or New England rum. It was the universal practice of the first settlers, and it was used by them on all occasions.

Skipper Davis went below and mixed himself a hearty draught of black strap (a mixture of rum and molasses) came on deck and
gave his orders to get under way. David did
the best he could to help, but invariably getting in the way. The orders of the Skipper
were Greek to him, so he went round after
Jack getting a tail hold when he could.

The boat filled away from the wharf, then
keeping her off to head down the river, when
over came the foresail and almost knocked
the daylights out of David, notwithstanding
the Skipper's warnings to look out for it.
The wind was blowing a fresh breeze, the air
was exhilarating and the trees along the banks
of the river clothed in verdure. The scene was
a pleasure and a delight to David. The boat
running before the wind, winged out, or as
Skipper Davis defined it, "cross legged and
split open."

Jack went below to get breakfast, and the

Skipper called David aft and began to give him a nautical catechism. He would occasionally take a bottle out of the binnacle for a pull at it. The nautical phrases that the Skipper used were all beyond David's comprehension. Then Jack came on deck to take the tiller, and the Skipper went below to breakfast. When he had finished, he relieved Jack and David and Jack breakfasted together. After clearing up the cuddy and making all tidy, they went on deck. The morning breeze was dying out and before noon it was calm.

The skipper was in a fair way for the rum to get the better of him again when they anchored off Parker's Flats. His tongue got thick and his senses were fast leaving him, when he called David to administer the Neptune oath to make a sailor of him in due form: "You, David Robertson, will never row when you can sail, will never walk when

you can ride, will never kiss the maid when
you can the mistress.   When you are boarded
by Neptune and he wants to know if you are
one of his subjects, you tell him you took the
oath off Parker's Flats in 1828 administered
by Skipper Davis." The Skipper then said it
was his watch below and turned in.

After dinner the wind breezed up to the
southwest, which was a fair wind and Jack
said, "It's too bad to lay here.   If we could
start now, we would be home by sunset.   I
have a good mind to try it." After talking
the matter over for half an hour or more,
Jack concluded to start and abide the conse-
quences.   They got the anchor and filled
away.   The boat was forty tons, and Jack felt
the responsibility of his situation with only
David to help, who hardly knew which end
went first, but with a fair wind and daylight
he could hardly go wrong.

After passing Seguin, they found a heavy

swell heaving in from sea. David turned pale but said nothing. Presently with his head over the rail, he was emptying his stomach overboard. They soon reached smoother water under the lea of Damiscove Islands. when David felt better. The wind that had been fresh was now moderating. A bank of fog was heaving up in the southeast which was causing Jack some uneasiness. After passing the Damiscoves, he steered for Pemaquid which he made all right.

It was now night and the fog had shut in. and he sent David below to call the Skipper. His eight hours sleep below had sobered him. but when he turned out, he was as dry as a fish. He was surprised and astonished when he came on deck and Jack showed him Pemaquid. At ten o'clock they were at anchor off Skipper Davis' house. They set the Skipper ashore, then Jack and David turned in on board the boat.

The next day they hauled in to the wharf and discharged the freight. The Skipper with his friend the Commodore were first on the wharf. soon followed by the neighbors, where hand shaking and familiar greetings were ex-changed. Each one had to look after his freight as it was hoisted out, and settle his bill with the Skipper.

After discharging, Jack and David went to the Skipper's house to get their dinner. David's bashfulness or rustic modesty made him uncomfortable. When he went into the house, Aunt Nancy passed him a chair. He sat down on the edge of the chair, put his feet on the rounds. hung down his head, acting awkward and gawky. Aunt Nancy pitied him and did the best she could to make him com-fortable. The dinner was soon ready and the invitation was given to "set by." When David took his chair to the table, he did not place it near enough, and did not know what

to do with his hands. Aunt Nancy helped
him with more than a liberal supply of wholesome viands. David was as hungry as a bear.
He was cutting up his beef in junks nearly
the size of his mouth, when an accident
occurred—his plate was near the edge of the
table, when he upset it and the contents were
spilled with his cup of tea at the same time
on Aunt Nancy's white floor. His face
turned red, the same hue as the Skipper's
nose. The Skipper and Jack roared with
laughter at this ludicrous scene.

David left the table, but the loving kindness
and tenderness of Aunt Nancy were soon
manifest. She picked up the beef and potatoes, wiped up the floor and said to David,
"You never mind a little accident like that."
After some persuasion she got him back to
the table, succeeding in getting him near
enough to the table this time, to avoid similar
accidents. Owing to David's bashfulness he

did not eat half as much as he wanted. Aunt Nancy tried to coax him to eat more, but he said he had eaten all he wanted, which was the biggest lie he ever told in his life.

After Jack had finished his dinner he went on board the boat leaving David, saying to him, "You can do the chores for Aunt Nancy." Seeing a lot of uncut wood in the dooryard, he took the axe and went at it, working away cutting the wood until Aunt Nancy called him to supper, which he managed to eat without any accident, but keeping his taciturn manner because it was natural to him.

After supper he went to the spring and brought the water and night's wood with plenty of kindling. He was tired and sleepy. Aunt Nancy showed him to a neat and cosy chamber under the eaves of the cottage, saying in her pleasant way, "Good night, David, don't get up until breakfast is ready, then I will call you."

On the following morning David was up with the Sun. He went down to the kitchen and was making the fire when Aunt Nancy got up. David was not only willing but glad to help her in any way he could with the breakfast. Aunt Nancy had already begun to appreciate his character and to regard him with an affection which was reciprocated by David.

The Skipper and his house were getting old, and some parts of the cottage needed repairing. David was born a natural mechanic. He spent the day doing odd jobs for Aunt Nancy about the cottage, which was congenial to him, besides being a pleasure to Aunt Nancy to have things fixed, which had been out of repair more or less for years.

It was night when Skipper Davis came home. He had bought sea-boots, oil skins and a sou'wester for David, and said to him, " We are getting ready for a fishing trip and

expect to sail tomorrow for the banks." The
cruise generally lasted four or five weeks. It
was the usual practice of the fishermen's
boats of the class of Skipper Davis' to make
two trips or fares to the banks in the summer
months. In the spring and fall they went
shore fishing and hauled up in the winter.
When the boats were fitted out for the banks,
they were loaded with their outfits as deep as
on their return with fish.

Skipper Davis' crew of six men were all
old hands and had been with him to the banks
for years and had never failed of getting a
fare of fish. On board vessels at sea the captain's authority is absolute, depending on his
own will, but on board a fisherman, although
the skipper has charge, he consults his crew,
because their interests are mutual. They
obey his orders when underway or going to
or from the fishing ground. When employed
in fishing all are anxious to get a fare of fish

and everyone does as he pleases, Jack being as good as his master.

Anchored on the banks, rolling and pitching for weeks, the scene is monotonous, in heavy weather and dark nights weird, gloomy and dismal, looking forward with a longing for the last hamper of salt to be wet, when they can start for home. On Sunday when there are other fishermen in their vicinity, they visit each other (which fishermen call coveing) spending the day swapping yarns, or telling of their remarkable adventures by sea and land. One of the principal amusements they have is spinning yarns (instead of wool they use froth) and they are always ready to swear to them as facts.

One of Skipper Davis' men was known as Captain Ben. He could spin more yarns than any other man in the State of Maine, and was always received as a welcome visitor on board the fishermen. According to his story he had sailed the world round in every capacity from cabin boy to commodore.

Here is an illustration of one of his yarns: Capt. Ben said, "When I was mate of the ship Albion, we were scudding out a typhoon in the China sea when I took the wheel, not daring to trust a man aboard to steer her. I saw a big sea coming and said to the Captain, 'Look out there! That sea is a going to poop this ship.' When the sea struck her I landed in the cat harpings with ten feet of the rudder head, and all of the stearing apparatus. The Captain sang out, 'Hard up, hard up! Mister Ben, for God's sake! * * * What is the use of harding up when I have got the wheel up here with me.''

Skipper Davis excelled in navigation, which was exceptional in skippers of fishermen of those times. Marine clocks had not been invented and each skipper provided himself with a watch which was indispensible to him.

Skipper Davis was considered to be a man of great ability by the fishermen on account of his nautical science. When he came on deck with his quadrant to get the true time or hour as indicated by the sun's passage over the meridian, it was more than the average fisherman could comprehend. The name invariably given to his instrument was the Skipper's hog yoke.

CHAPTER IV

BEFORE the time came for David to go on board, Aunt Nancy had got a fit-out for David. She had got a sea chest that once belonged to the Skipper, putting in a bed quilt and pillow, besides clothes, stockings and mittens, with a box containing buttons, needles and thread. When he started to go, Aunt Nancy bade him good bye with a benediction of "God bless you, David." He responded in his homely way, his heart overflowing with gratitude. It was a beautiful June day, a warm, gentle, south wind blowing, and the sun radiant and shining when Skipper Davis filled away bound for Castine. The way led through a labyrinthal passage leaving islands on either side, mostly covered with evergreen trees of a primitive growth with beautiful beaches, diversified with ledges and boulders. The scenery was fascinating and delightful.

David looking on these sylvan islands for the first time conceived the idea of making one his home. Skipper Davis arrived at Castine that evening, where he found old acquaintances in abundance. There were twenty or more fishermen fitting out for the banks, including a full rigged ship discharging a cargo of salt—Castine being at that time the largest port in eastern Maine for fishermen's outfits. Flocking around Skipper Davis were the fishermen listening to his familiar talk or conversation and enjoying his social company, they regarding him as the Patriarch of the fishing fleet of Maine. There is a genial and social friendship existing among fishermen. They sympathize with one another in misfortune and rejoice with each other in prosperity. A more free-

FRENCHMAN'S BAY—POINT OF DEPARTURE FOR THE BANKS.

hearted people do not exist than the fishermen on the coast of Maine.

The next day Skipper Davis took on board
the salt and stores, and sailed for the banks
early the next morning, with several fishermen in company. Before losing sight of Mt.
Desert he had also lost sight of the rest of
the fishermen, as Skipper Davis always sailed
by his own compass.

On the third day after leaving Castine the
Skipper got soundings on Brown's bank.
Soon after sounding he sighted a fisherman at
anchor. He ran down and spoke him when
the following soliloquy was heard:

" Boat ahoy!"

" Halloo!"

" Getting any fish?"

" Yes, walloping cod for hauling!"

Skipper Davis giving him a berth, let go
the anchor, brought her up with fifty fathoms
in the hawse, took in the foresail, and balance

reefed the mainsail. Everything being in readiness all hands were soon employed a-fishing.

David was seasick, but got his line overboard with the rest and soon caught his first fish. The excitement of hauling fish, notwithstanding his seasickness, exhilarated him. David asked Capt. Ben, if he did not call it rough. "Rough!" exclaimed Capt. Ben, "It is as smooth as a cat's back. Rough! When I was only ten years old I went to the western banks with Skipper Thompson. It was so rough on the banks that skipper Tom nailed my coat tails to the deck and made me eat out of my hat."

It took nearly four weeks to wet the salt. It was the middle of July when the Skipper gave orders to heave ahead, which was received with a hearty welcome. Then off for home with a hard full.

> " From gray sea fog, from icy drift,
> From peril and from pain,
> The home-bound fisher greets thy lights,
> O hundred harbored Maine!"   *Whittier.*

After a short and pleasant passage, with ensign flying they rounded to and once more came ashore off Skipper Davis' cottage, when they received the greetings of friends and neighbors. They expressed themselves in the dialect of those times with "How fares ye? Welcome home! Fish or no fish? Welcome home Skipper Davis!"

Jack and David hauled the boat into the wharf to prepare or make ready to "wash out" (the term invariably used by fishermen when discharging fish). The next three days Skipper Davis and his crew were employed discharging and getting ready to sail again for the banks. The quicker they could get away the better, as by this means they hoped to get a fare of fish before the equinoxial gales in September.

The September gale which often happens about the time the sun crosses the equator is the dread and fear of all bank fishermen.

The statistics, or collection of facts, show that the September gales have made desolate many a hearth in the cottage homes of the New England fishermen.

Skipper Davis, like his boat, was growing old. He dreaded to go this cruise, but stern necessity, including want, need and poverty compelled him. His irregular and intemperate life had been wasteful and extravagant. He now bitterly repented the follies of his past life—but now too late. With his best foot forward, and hard on to seventy years of age, he once more goes on board for Castine. After getting his supply of salt and stores, then off and away for the banks.

Arriving on the banks the first of August, there seemed to be a pleasing prospect of filling up by the first of September. In the third week in August he had wet more than three quarters of the salt, when it began to thicken up. The clouds looked heavy with a

leaden hue, and the air was thick and hazy.
Skipper Davis' countenance showed anxiety.

"What do you think of the weather, Capt.
Ben?" asked the Skipper.   "I think it is
going to be a snorter," replied Capt. Ben.

There was but little wind, but a heavy sea
was rolling in from the southeast.   "Heave
ahead my hearties, and sight the anchor," were
the orders of Skipper Davis.   Sighting the
anchor to be sure it was clear, they then let it
go again and paid out a hundred fathoms
of hawser, put everything below that was
movable, put the tarpauling on the hatches,
and battered them down.   The foresail was
unbent and put below, the mainsail was furled
and a storm trysail set for a riding sail.

When they had made all secure, the gale
came on gradually, each puff stronger than
the preceding one.   At sundown the gale
was increasing.   They shut the cuddy as tight
as possible.   The sea piled on the decks until

they could hold no more. Skipper Davis'
greatest anxiety was that the boat would
spring aleak, but if she kept tight she would
weather out the gale. It is hard to imagine
how the men felt that night shut up in the
cuddy of the boat, with the chances more
than equal for them never to see another sunrise.

The summer gales are short, and the next
forenoon at ten o'clock the sun was out and
shining brightly. After dinner all hands were
fishing as if nothing had happened.

It was a joyful day on board the Chebacco
boat when the salt was used up. Even Capt.
Ben in spite of his age was manifesting hilar-
ity by dancing a double shuffle on deck.
Skipper Davis brought up the jug of New
England rum and put it on the binnacle and
said, "Drink hearty, boys, and give the old
boat a good name."

Each one stepped up to drink according to

his seniority, Capt. Ben leading the van. When he took the jug he proposed this sentiment: " Here's to the ship that goes—the wind that blows—and the lass that loves a sailor."

When all hands had taken a pull at the jug except David, Capt. Ben said to David, " Don't you never touch it, my lad. If it had not been for that jug, I would have walked the quarter deck of a seventy-four gun ship, with more brass buttons on my coat than there are points of the compass. If you think this yarn is spun of wool you ask Skipper Davis or Commodore Tucker."

It was pleasant weather and with a fair wind they soon arrived home from the banks. After washing out, it was necessary to haul the boat ashore to scrape the barnacles off her bottom, preparatory to shore fishing. When shore fishing they were devoid of that uneasy or painful apprehension of danger,

because they were not exposed to the hazard
and the peril of the banks, for the reason
that they could make a harbor in heavy
weather.

Skipper Davis was a pilot and well acquainted with all the harbors in eastern Maine.
When anchored on the fishing ground and
their labor in getting fish crowned with success, they would be loth to leave the ground,
and hold on as long as possible. In heavy
weather, when it came on too tough under
reefed sails they would make a harbor.

At such times Skipper Davis would give
the old Chebacco boat hearty victuals, with
the laconic phrase of "Boys, she is all white
oak." It was blue times indeed when the old
boat could not make a harbor under double
reefed sails.

Skipper Davis when he made a harbor
made a good one. When they anchored under
the lee of one of the islands that form the

SETTING SAIL FOR THE BANKS.

harbors of the Maine coast, where their boat lay snug and close, no matter how hard the storm raged, it brought no care to them as they were completely sheltered. They could sympathize with the old deacon at the village prayer meeting when he exclaimed, " Brothers and sisters, I feel it is good for me to be here."

In the cosy cuddy of the boat with a good fire in the fire-place, the Skipper would mount his hobby horse telling the biographical incidents of the Commodore with variations, followed by Capt. Ben, who spun yarns that were an improvement on Sinbad or the flying Dutchman.

It was getting late in November and the weather was showery, when by mutual consent they went home and hauled up the boat in her winter quarters. The season had been a prosperous one. After the fish had been sold and a settlement made David's share was more than a hundred dollars. He was going

to live with the Skipper, go to school and care
for the old folks.

Skipper Davis was one of the most successful fishermen in Maine. He and his boat
would make from eight to ten hundred dollars
a year, but he had no aptitude for business.
He had more generosity than wisdom. He
would live extravagantly while his money
lasted and when it was gone, live extravagantly
on credit. Sharpers cheated him, and now
he was afflicted with rheumatism and old age.
His boat like the Skipper had seen her best
days and the cottage had become dilapidated,
but in spite of all he was cheerful, consoling
himself with the thought that there was an
even chance for something to turn in his favor,
but he did not know what.

Skipper Davis was not an exception to
mariners in general. They made money and
spent it. If by some chance they escape the
perils of their hazardous life and live to old

THE ROMANTIC STORY OF DAVID ROBERTSON.   51

age, not one in twenty has a competency.
Then they learn that charity begins and ends
at home.

Before David could go to school one of the
first things to be done was to get winter
clothes for him, so a woman tailor was
employed to come to the house to make him
a winter suit to wear to school. When buy-
ing the cloth, Aunt Nancy, the woman tailor
and even the Skipper took counsel together
on the merits of the cloth. The woman
gray, the Skipper blue. and it was finally
settled by arbitration. David himself being
umpire.

In due time the clothes were ready and the
following Monday Aunt Nancy had him ready
for school, but for some cause he looked awkward. His arm were too long, and he had
his suspenders too tight. which made his
trousers too short; his head was on one side,
his sandy hair was thick and was cut round in

a circle showing less than two inches of his forehead. Aunt Nancy tried her best to get him in shape, but had to give it up as hopeless, soliloquizing, "There, there, well, I can't help it, he is the best boy that ever lived."

David with Aunt Nancy's satchel containing his books and dinner set out for school. If perseverance had not been a leading trait in his character, he would have abandoned the idea of school because of his bashfulness. He did not mind the boys so much, but the girls were a sore trouble to him. If one of them spoke to him, he would blush so that the freckles on his face would turn red.

David was attentive and studious at school, and notwithstanding his rustic manners, he had the respect of the teacher.

Among the scholars there was a boy older than David that was droll and a mimic. He made sport of David, with low jests, and tried to make him appear ridiculous. David for a

time took no notice, but after awhile forbear-
ance ceased to be a virtue.   David's Scotch-
Irish temper got the advantage of him, when
he took the droll by the shoulders and said,
"I have a good mind to shake you!" making
good his threat until he shook the breath out
of him, then said to him, "If you do not stop
it, I will shake you again."

David had a natural aptitude to conform to
the situation in which he was placed and do
what was necessary without being told; making the skipper and his wife comfortable,
which was a mutual pleasure to the old folks
and to David.

CHAPTER V

IT was a hot campaign in 1828 when Jackson and Adams were the candidates for the Presidency of the United States. The political parties manifested hard feeling against one another, both north and south.

The Commodore and the Skipper did not agree in their political opinions and many was the hard fought combat they had together. The Commodore would stand by his guns, swearing like a pirate, converting the Skipper and it generally took an hour or more to make the Skipper haul down his colors. But the conversion was not of long continuance. The next time they came together, the Skipper would hurrah for Jackson, when the Commodore would have to convert him over again. The Commodore was victorious, because

every vote in the town was for the Adams'
ticket.   When the news was received of
Jackson's election, the Skipper with manifes-
tations of patriotic joy, shouted, "Hurrah for
Jackson." The Commodore said, "D——d
him, he wasn't half converted."

The winter wore away.   David was a
greater favorite than ever with the Skipper
and Aunt Nancy, humoring the Skipper in
his garrulity and sympathizing with him when
he had an attack of rheumatism, not by
loquacity but actions, and he was truly a help
to them in their old age.

The vernal season, spring, had come, the
time to start the old chebacco boat.   A consultation was held between the Skipper, Capt.
Ben and Jack considering what was best;
whether to fit the boat for the banks or have
her go shore fishing.   It would involve con-
siderable expense to fit her away.   She would
have to be recalked and have a new mainsail.

Talking the matter over for and against, they decided to send her one trip to the banks and the rest of the season shore fishing.

It had been the practice for years to send the boat up the Kennebec river before going to the banks, to get the necessary outfits of all that was needful, excepting salt and bait, which were got at Castine.

After calking and painting the boat, the Skipper, Jack and David in the old boat, sailed for the Kennebec. The neighbors all had well founded confidence in Skipper Davis and sent by him what they had to sell or exchange for West India goods. He could always do better for them than they could for themselves, owing to a business firm that the Skipper had done business with many years, who looked after him and his interest.

Arriving at the river town, David had an incessant craving to go home to see his mother. Getting the consent of the Skipper early next morning, he set out on his journey, and was once more on the river road, this time on the right road and going the right way.

When he got to the clearing where the woman had given him the bread and cheese, he went to the door and rapped, and the identical woman came to the door. She knew him and invited him in. David said, "I came to pay you for the bread and cheese." He laid down a Spanish milled dollar against her protest, said good by and was off. She said to herself, "Cast thy bread on the waters for thou shalt find it after many days."

David trudged on his journey, arriving at his old home about two o'clock. He saw his father and brothers in the field plowing. Everything looked the same, excepting the new house which was up, boarded and shingled. The door to the log house was open, and when he stepped on the threshold his mother was standing back to the door, but when she heard his step she knew it was David. With ecstasy of joy, overflowing with happiness, she put both her arms round his neck with the exclamation, "O David!" If anything is pure it is the unchangeable love of a mother to her son.

After telling his mother his adventures, without going into details, he asked about his father, and taking from his pocket the money said, "Give this to father, it will help him lo complete the house." David respected his father, but the memory of scenes that were past he could forgive, but not forget. Then with a simple good by and God bless you, he was gone.

When Mr. Robertson came home, he found Mrs. Robertson sitting in her rocking chair, the baby in her lap and sobbing convulsively. Mr. Robertson said, "Why, what is the matter, mother?" She sobbed with audible grief,

"David has been home." Mr. Robertson's face betrayed emotion when he heard this, and he gave utterance to the single word, "David?" He had a heartfelt grief that the pen is inadequate to describe. The coals of fire that were heaped on his head were red hot. To see him suffering with sorrowful pangs and heartaches, a person must have been stone-hearted not to have pitied him.

It was midnight when David got back to the boat. The next day Jack and David took in the freight and stores. When the freight was all aboard it was night and Jack got supper. When David went to hunt up the Skipper he found him with half a dozen old codgers drinking at the Skipper's expense, to the health of Commodore Tucker and Andrew Jackson, but after some persuasion David got him to go with him on board. The Skipper made a crooked wake. David took him by the arm and he got along better. It took both Jack and David to get him on board and into his berth, when no more was heard from him until next morning.

When they started for home, on the way down river Skipper Davis had an attack of rheumatism and he claimed Medford rum and sulphur would cure the disease if taken often. Its effect upon him was to make him dozy, when he turned in. Jack and David sailed the boat home. After discharging the freight, all was in readiness for the trip to Castine excepting Skipper Davis, whose rheumatism was a sore trouble to him. He prescribed for himself the rum and sulphur which affected his head, while the rheumatism affected his joints and limbs. Very few physicians, if any, could diagnose his disease or distinguish which was the worse—the disease or the remedy.

After waiting ten days for Skipper Davis to get better, without improvement, he had to

SKIPPER DAVIS' CHEBACCO BOAT.

get Capt. Ben to take charge of the boat to go to the banks, not without some forebodings, but necessity has no choice. Capt. Ben sailed for Castine to get his salt and bait, also a new cable and then sailed for Brown's banks.*

Capt. Ben now having charge, he left off his trifling and frivolous manner. The crew missed Skipper Davis and also Capt. Ben's merriment. Coming events cast their shadows. It was a misty and lowery day when Captain Ben sailed for the banks, with the wind ahead, followed by calms and variables with plenty of rain. It was eight days after leaving Castine before Capt. Ben got soundings on Brown's banks.

According to the boat log which noted events as well as courses, distances, latitude, wind and departure, Capt. Ben arrived on the

*This bank is call Brown's bank by all fishermen, but the true name is Blonde bank.

banks two days before Skipper Davis sailed
for home with a full fare of fish the year
before. The spring school of fish had gone
from the banks when Capt. Ben arrived this
time. They tried hard for fish but without
success, shifting berths every day, trying all
over the banks, sometimes in sight of Cape
Sable and then shifting to the extreme edge in
deep water. They found plenty of dog fish,
the curse of all fishermen. Capt. Ben said
they never made their appearance on the banks
before until July. They spent a fortnight
in vain, not averaging a quintal of fish a day.

On the following Sunday, Capt. Ben got
an observation of the sun, by this means getting the true time and latitude, which he
found was 43 degrees, 10 minutes, saying,
"La Have is due east sixty miles." The wind
was southwest. By mutual consent they got
under way and were off for La Have bank.
At ten o'clock the same night they got sound-

ings on the bank in fifty fathoms, this being the shoalest water on La Have bank. They anchored with seventy-five fathoms of cable and turned in excepting the watch.

They spent a week on the bank without getting any fish. Capt. Ben was discouraged. A gloom and sadness were manifest among the crew of the old chebacco boat that had never failed before to bring home a fare of fish. There is a superstition among sailors and fishermen; they firmly believe in luck and fate. Capt. Ben said "It was the thirteenth. day of July when we left Castine, and it was Friday when we left home, but boys let us stick to it as long as there is a shot in the locker or Indian meal enoug to stir up a Johnny cake."

Northwest from La Have bank thirty-five miles lay Roseway bank. Capt. Ben and his crew thought it was best to try there before giving up and once more try fortune—luck or chance for fish. It was night when they got under way for Roseway bank. Arriving the next morning they anchored on the bank in thirty fathoms of water before their line got bottom. They got cod fish and a hard day's work was done on board the old boat that day. They hauled fish until the kits or checker board* could hold no more. It took most of the night to dress them down.

The next morning there was a heavy sea, the wind southeast and fresh, the fish biting sharp with the sea making and the wind increasing. Capt. Ben was loth to stop fishing, wishing to make up for lost time and now getting large cod fish. Thinking the wind was nothing but a summer breeze and expecting it to moderate, they kept on fishing until the decks were full of fish. They hardly realized how bad it was, they were so anxious

---

*On deck of a fisherman when fishing, the deck is divided in checks by planks made and fitted for the purpose, called by the fishermen the checker board.

to get fish. The wind was blowing a brisk gale, increasing to sudden gusts, assuming the violence of a hurricane. The sea came aboard, obliging them to put on the hatches and make them secure. Capt. Ben told David and the crew to go below and shut the companion slide and doors. Capt. Ben and Jack lashed themselves to the masts. The fish had washed overboard, the deck was full to the rails of water, and the boat rolling and pitching in a terrible manner, while Jack and Capt. Ben looked on with dread and sorrow, watching her for an hour or more.

At length Capt. Ben saw a big sea coming and sung out to Jack to hold on. He got the axe and sprang for the jaws of the fore gaff and none too soon, for the old boat with a plunge went out of sight. When she came up everything was gone from her deck including the waist boards and wherries*. The cable

---

*A light boat used at that time.

tier that was on deck was tailing out astern.
There had been a strain on every butt and
seam, proving that the craft was built of oak
and copper fastened. When she went under
she shook and trembled from stem to stern.

At sea there are invariably three heavy seas
following in succession in hard gales of wind.
With the experience that Capt. Ben had, he
knew there were two more to come and he
did not believe the old boat could stand the
pressure, so with one blow he cut the cable.
When the boat fell off the trysail now got
the full force of the gale.   It split from clue
to earing.   Capt. Ben, nimble as a boy, got
aft and took the tiller, keeping her before the
gale, scudding her under bare poles.   It was
coming on night and the old boat driving
before the gale at a fearful rate.   The binnacle and compass were gone and they now had
no means of knowing the exact way the gale
of wind was blowing.   Capt. Ben judged the

CHEBACCO BOAT SCUDDING OUT A GALE.

gale or hurricane to be east southeast, and Cape Sable was bearing west northwest, dis- tance thirty-five miles, when he cut the cable, making proper allowance for variation. If the gale continued four hours longer and his reckoning was right, she would be ashore on Cape Sable. If the wind veered to the north she would scud by Cape Sable and go clear.

It was six o'clock by Capt. Ben's bull's eye watch when he cut the cable. It was now nine o'clock and before ten she would be ashore or go by. It was dark as pitch, the air full of water, caused by the hurricane blowing the foam or spray off the seas. Capt. Ben was powerless but thought the chance about equal for her to scud by Cape Sable. Language is inadequate to describe the feelings of the men, with alternate hopes and fears. Capt. Ben said, "My reckoning is up and the next ten minutes will decide our fate."

The strain now brought to bear on the

minds of those men was as much as human nature could stand, and only those who have been in a similar situation can fully understand their feelings—now with anxious care waiting for uncertain or inevitable fate to decide their destiny, when an unexpected occurrence took place. Suddenly and only for a minute it was stark calm, when the wind with an impetuous and sudden gust was blowing from the opposite direction with equal velocity, the old boat scudding now for the Atlantic Ocean, with sea room of more than three thousand miles.

Free now from imminent danger, with hopes revived, they were comparatively cheerful. The morning light was hailed with joy, and the sun rose clear. Capt. Ben still at the tiller, lashed, with the boat scudding ten knots at least, the tremendous seas washing over her, as if she was a half tide ledge. With all their misfortunes they had the satisfaction

and consolation that the weather was moderating, and the old boat was tight.   Capt. Ben
said she was scudding about sou'southeast,
making use of the sun for his compass.   The
cook of the boat after various and unsuccessful attempts to make coffee had at last succeeded, and with a quart pot was trying to
get it aft to Capt. Ben, and by dint of perse-
vering, at last succeeded.   Like nectar to the
Gods, were victuals and drink to Capt. Ben.

It had now moderated so much that they
two-reefed the foresail, and let. her come to
the wind.   Capt. Ben got the latitude at noon,
making her in 42 degrees, 20 minutes, Cape
Sable bearing north by west seventy miles.
They lay by until past three o'clock, then set
the mainsail double reefed, hauled the sheets
flat aft and the old boat was off, heading for
the Maine coast, somewhere between Sacca-
rap and Quoddy, on the starboard* tack for

*The word larboard is obsolete, port being substituted.

fifteen hours. It was still blowing hard, the boat smothering to it full and by under double reefs, Capt. Ben judging by the north star, that the wind was about north.

The next morning the wind westerned, when they tacked to the eastward. At noon the latitude was 43 degrees, 40 minutes, Mt. Desert rock bearing nor'west by west thirty-five miles by estimation, the wind moderating, and the sea going down. The wind backened to the northward, blowing a whole-sail breeze with starboard tacks aboard.

The old boat was now doing her best for Pemaquid, and before daybreak the next morning they made the light on Monhegan, proving that the boat had outrun Capt. Ben's reckoning. He could almost instinctively find his way home the darkest night that ever was, having fished the ground over for years.

It may seem strange that Capt. Ben had formed an attachment for the boat. She had carried him safely through so many dangers, seen and unseen, and had been his home spring, summer and fall for ten years. By her he had gained his sustenance, now coming home without a fare of fish for the first time. The old boat had brought her wings, but had lost her tail feathers.

The expense of fitting out the boat was more than it ever had been before, and the prospect to go shore fishing to get money enough to pay the bank outfits, besides having to repair the boat's damages was anything but pleasing. Capt. Ben had done the best and all that he could, but would neither get censure or praise.

At noon that day, they were in sight of Pemaquid, the dearest spot on earth to Capt. Ben. In years gone by whenever they returned from fishing, the sight of Pemaquid was hailed with gladness and gaiety, with ensign flying and boat "scuppers to" with fish.

Now with grief and sadness they came in sight of home, the old boat almost a wreck, without fish. Was it luck or destiny? It seemed to Capt. Ben while meditating dejectedly that it was the decree of fate that he would have to go with Skipper Davis hand in hand, over the hill to the poor house the coming winter.

CHAPTER VI

S KIPPER Davis with anxious care and uneasiness had been waiting for the boat's return a fortnight; every day found him down on Pemaquid Point with a spyglass on the lookout. He could tell her as far as his vision extended, among a hundred. When at last he recognized her, it animated him so for the time being he forgot his rheumatism, and swung his tarpaulin hat, with a cry of exultation, "Hurrah for old Hickory." Watching the boat with close attention as she approached, when he saw her waist and boats were gone, with no ensign flying, it told him the whole story. She was now near enough for him to distinguish the men on board; with the glass he espied David and soliloquized, " Thank God, David is alive; he is the best boy that ever gutted a fish." He then trudged sadly home speculating on the gloomy prospects.   The old boat got to her anchorage off Skipper Davis' cottage before night, and let go her sheet anchor (the fishing anchor was on Roseway bank).

When Capt. Ben went ashore, he was met by Skipper Davis, who reached out his hand and took Capt. Ben's, and with a hearty shake said: " How fares ye?   Welcome home, Capt. Ben, don't look so down-hearted, and cheer up.   As long as I can catch a fish I will divide with you, and cut him fore and aft, not athwart ships giving you the tail."

The old hero of the Revolution, Tucker, was present at the meeting of Capt. Ben and Skipper Davis; the Commodore was solving a mathematical problem, mentally dividing his meagre pension of twenty dollars a month into three parts and using somewhat irreverent language, when he accosted the Skipper,

" You and Ben catch the fish, and I will raise the potatoes and divide the pension and we will never surrender or haul down the flag so long as we can keep afloat."

Skipper Davis, Capt. Ben and Jack consulted together contriving the ways and means to get what was necessary for the boat before she could go shore fishing, taking an inventory and then computing the necessary expense. The consultation made them hesitate. The summary or brief computation as follows: The heavy bill up the Kennebec for provision, the salt, bait, cable and mainsail at Castine, the calking and painting at home; and what they would have to obtain, viz.: fishing cable, anchor, boats, compass, binnacle and fishing gear, besides a carpenter's bill for putting on a waist and making kits.

It seemed almost against fate to start the old boat under the circumstances, when the best of the fishing season was gone. They thought they could do nothing better and went on board the next day for Castine, concluding to look for their money where they lost it with a presentiment in their minds of calamity or misfortune.

When they arrived at Castine, Skipper Davis with his threadbare clothes well patched by Aunt Nancy, with a careworn countenance went to the outfit merchant to furnish him what was needed for the boat. The merchant did not want to increase his bill without security (he fully understood the Skipper's situation), which obliged Skipper Davis to give a bottomry bond of the boat, making the old adage true, that has been handed down from antiquity that "misfortune never comes alone." Skipper Davis firmly believed in luck, it had been a part of his nature at all times, and in all circumstances, but was now to learn that a fish does not always belong to the man that catches him.

With hurry and disorder, without stopping to consider, with his mind occupied wholly with the one idea of getting fish to relieve him from his trouble, not using good judgment, getting more or less than was necessary for the boat, the once jolly Skipper was now fretful and peevish (except when under the influence of a stimulant) and became capricious.

There was not a chance in ten for them to get fish enough in two months, to pay the Castine bills when the bottomery bond expired. The outlook was discouraging, but the Skipper mindful of his great successes in years that were gone could not, or would not believe that luck, fate or chance, that had always been in his favor, would forsake him now. With his visionary and whimsical scheme in his head when he arrived on the fishing ground, for the next four weeks they tried hard for fish between Grand Manan and

Monhegan, making the mistake of changing the fishing ground too often.

The Skipper having more anxiety than patience at last became discouraged and gave up the fight. With too much care, he aged rapidly under his misfortunes, and looked ten years older than when he left Pemaquid. Wearied in body and mind Skipper Davis and his crew were downcast and dejected.

After fishing the month of September with poor success, their provisions were most gone. They abandoned the undertaking and returned to Castine. The merchant at Castine was of the old school and a gentleman. It was de-nominated in the bottomry bond that he had of Skipper Davis, that in case of failure to pay the bond at the expiration of the time specified he was to deliver the boat at Castine.

Skipper Davis was the soul of honor and under no circumstances would he betray his trust or even equivocate to save the boat.* On his arrival at Castine the Skipper with tottering steps delivered the boat's papers to the merchant, who handed them back, saying, " I would rather lose my money than take your boat. You may take the boat home, when I call for her will be time enough to deliver her."

Skipper Davis and his crew went home in the old boat. The Skipper's ambition was

---

*Many of the fishermen of those times were noted for their observance of the truth. When the treaty was concluded between the English Dominion of Nova Scotia and the United States, the agreement provided that the fishermen of the Independent States should take no fish inside of three miles of the shores of Nova Scotia. The fishermen to get fresh bait would set their nets inside of the limits to catch herring when they could not get them on the fishing ground. The English cutter or Revenue boat would often speak the Yankee fishermen and inquire where they got their bait. If they replied on the ground, no more notice was taken of the matter. The cutter spoke Capt. Burgess who belonged to one of the island towns in Penobscot Bay, hailing him with the formal question, "Where did you get your bait!" Capt. Burgess was loth to answer and would not say he caught them on the ground. He was taken out and his vessel towed to Halifax or some other Nova Scotia port, his vessel and fish confiscated, then left to get home the best he could. When questioned about the affair his answer was, " Do you think I would lie for an old vessel?"

gone now; worn out and sick, he had nothing
to look forward to or cheer his drooping
spirits. When he arrived home, he was too
feeble to walk. David took him by the arm
and led him home. His curls that hung down
on his shoulders had turned from gray to
white. Notwithstanding his venerable appearance, he had the pleasing look of childhood, sitting in his arm chair now almost
helpless. He would at times hold Aunt
Nancy's hand in deep thought, knowing in his
heart that she had done him good, not evil, all
the days of her life, living with him as con-
sort in unity for more than forty years.

It was Skipper Davis' last sickness. All
that a kind heart and hands could do Aunt
Nancy did for him. He had lived the age
allotted to man, when the summons came.
He died with a pleasant smile on his countenance, with quiet submission. It was a beautiful, still autumn day when friends and

neighbors far and near followed the remains
of Skipper Davis to his last resting place in
the church-yard burying ground.

There is something grand and noble in the
companionship of husband and wife, who
have lived together many years in harmony.
Broken hearted now was Aunt Nancy, following skipper Davis to the grave, her tears min-
gling with the dust of the road, with sad
expressions of sorrow from the cottage to the
church-yard. She had walked with him down
the hard path of life for forty years, and
would wait patiently for the time when she
could lie side by side with him in the burying
ground.

Capt. Ben, who all his life was as free as
water with his money, was now without a
dollar or a home, bowed down with age, and
the cold icy winter near at hand. He had
braved the dangers of the sea and oceans for
sixty years, as now, without an enemy or

friend in the wide world, he went over the hill to be supported at the public expense.

A sincere affection Capt. Ben had for Skipper Davis. He went to the grave and looked at Skipper Davis in his coffin with a pang of sorrow, lingering there until the lid was closed that fastened Skipper Davis down forever. With honest tears on his weather-beaten cheeks he slowly and moodily walked away, wishing himself lying beside Skipper Davis.

The situation in which David now found himself, with nothing to his credit for his summer fishing, left on his own resources with Aunt Nancy in the dilapidated cottage, with the icy cold winter coming on, necessitated prompt action. He conceived the idea of going small boat fishing with Jack, who made his home in the cuddy of the old boat that was hauled up in her winter quarters, and would probably remain there until next spring.

When David mentioned to Jack his idea to go small boat fishing, and asked him to go with him, Jack, although an honest heart beat under his blue flannel shirt, had not the capacity of mind to manage or direct, and was submissive to David's judgment, whose intellect was far above Jack's. Thus with Jack's practical and David's theoretical knowledge, they were well adapted to go fishing together.

During the months of October and November David and Jack went small boat fishing every day when it was possible to fish, meeting with success beyond their expectations. They were indebted to Capt. Ben who went with them in pleasant weather, and showed them by marks and ranges the best fishing grounds. David was now able to aid and assist Aunt Nancy and keep the wolf from the door. The poverty that threatened them the coming winter had disappeared.

Aunt Nancy never recovered her cheerful and pleasant manner, doing her simple house work in a quiet and sedate way, showing plainly her deep grief and sadness. The cold, chill winds of December had come, which compelled David and Jack to stop fishing.

David's eccentric manner at times had a strange effect on those that did not understand his silent or taciturn ways. He and Aunt Nancy might be seen in the kitchen of the cottage in the long winter evenings, with Aunt Nancy sitting in her rocking chair thoughtful and meditative, while David, who was chary of his thoughts seldom gave them expression. He seemed to have an instinctive desire to do for Aunt Nancy what was essential and needful. If he had been her son it appeared to her that she could not have loved him more. She looked on him as sent by Divine Providence to comfort her in her great affliction.

In the sacred scriptures she had implicit faith, and was often thinking of a sentence in the holy writings as applied to her own situation. "I have been young, and now am old; yet have I not seen the righteous forsaken, nor his seed begging bread." It had been the habitual practice for years for the young folks to meet at Skipper Davis' cottage on winter evenings, and listen to the jovial skipper or Capt. Ben's sea stories of by-gone days. The once cheerful cottage was now forsaken by its former associates, for the reason that Aunt Nancy was no company for them now. Aunt Nancy was noted for her social and agreeable ways towards the young people, and beloved by them. They would occasionally make her a short visit, bringing her some delicacy or dainty which she would receive with gratitude, manifested by a pleasant smile.

She knew her days were numbered, and would be glad to receive the welcome message, having a firm belief in immortality. Her disease or complaint baffled the skill of the physicians, their drugs and blood letting did her no good. She had given up. The sorrow on which her mind was continually dwelling, with a strong desire to die, brought about the final result. The body or system when deprived of hope, which keeps body and soul together, soon separate under these conditions.

Aunt Nancy died of grief, broken hearted. The fleeting days of cold winter had gone. It was early spring when the Divine command was made for Aunt Nancy, who died with heavenly consolation, with words of faith and hope on her lips, and was laid by the side of Skipper Davis.

CHAPTER VII.

THERE were few dry eyes at the
funeral obsequies of Aunt Nancy.
One and all of her acquaintances, remember-
ing now the many kind acts she had done for
them when in sickness and trouble, felt it
incumbent on them to see her remains.
David walked home from the funeral thoughtful, with his mind confused, and now for the
first time in his life felt lonesome. Some of
the neighbors came in out of respect, some
for curiosity. Jack would have been pleased
to stay with him, but David showed by his
silence he would rather Jack would stay at
home. David passed the night alone in the
cottage, in deep meditation. In this mood, for
several days, David remained in the cottage,
much perplexed as to what his future course

should be. After a time he solved the problem, to his satisfaction, and soon after put it
into effect, as the sequel shows.

While David was living in the cottage,
an individual, claiming to be Aunt Nancy's
next of kin, came and carried away the furniture and all the movables against the protest
of Skipper Davis' creditors, not leaving even
a bed for David, acting on the principle that
" might makes right."

Aunt Nancy had often plainly expressed in
direct terms, that what she had or what she
left belonged to David. The whole neighborhood were indignant and thought it an imposi-
tion. The old hero, the Commodore, with
words that lacked reverence to Divinity, said
to Aunt Nancy's kinsman, "I would blow
you out of water, you hell-hound, if I had a
gun loaded," showing the metal the old hero
was made of. With flashing eyes that eighty-
three years had not dimmed he said, " You

ought to be keel-hauled you d——d land shark."

Aunt Nancy left an old Bible that had been her solace and comfort all the days of so many years. She had marked passages in the book from Genesis to Revelations, for David to read carefully and reflect on, after she was dead. David allowed Aunt Nancy's kinsman to carry off everything without remonstrance, except the Bible. In regard to that, David's countenance indexed his mind, and the kinsman had discretion enough to let the Bible alone. David had all the time there was, but not enough to get mad, as that would take six weeks, and six years to get over it.

David was a lover of nature. There was something implanted in him—a brooding tenderness toward all the human family, but enigmatical even to them that knew him best. When Aunt Nancy died she was not pecuniarily indebted to any one. David would not

permit her to be buried at the public expense.
For this reason he remained at Pemaquid, to
gain by labor at boat fishing money enough to
pay her funeral expenses. When he had accomplished his purpose he would bid farewell to Pemaquid, and carry his project into
effect.

David had built himself a wherry the past
winter, which was a model specimen of his
skill. In the months of May and June, David
went fishing with Jack in the wherry. He
then paid the debts, giving everyone his due
and had a small surplus in his pocket. He
started in the wherry with his meagre belongings, including a gun and pup, and sailed
away from Pemaquid early in the morning,
with fair weather on a beautiful July day,
leaving the cottage to go to ruin.

Poor Jack, who was known as Jack Froth
by the fishermen, would have sailed the world
around with David in the wherry, if given the

opportunity. Notwithstanding his honest heart his failing was his mouth, which was open on all occasions, his tongue running with perpetual motion from July to January. David had due sense of all the favors he had received from Jack, and would have divided his last dollar with him, but could not endure Jack's neverceasing talkativeness. More than that he did not think it would be for Jack's interest.

When Jack found David was gone, he took it to heart, and was pained at the manner in which he considered David had left him. A sincere attachment Jack had for David, which Jack thought was mutual. David's actions surprised him, and for once in his life his loquacity was at a full stop.

David sailed away to the eastward, leaving Georges Island on the starboard hand, then following the shore of St. George to Tenant's Harbor, thence to White Head, the entrance

to the Mussel Ridge channel. The way now
led in and out through mazy windings, leaving island after island mostly on the port hand.
The diversified appearance of these islands
covered with primal evergreen trees, fascinated him now more than ever on that delightful July day. The scenery thrilled him with
pleasing sensations. The sea fowl were beyond enumeration. With a single discharge
of his gun he killed six, and his young
retriever dog prompted by instinct, was quickly
after them.

The south wind was dying out, and the
western sun was about two hours high when
David landed on the shingle beach on one of
those bowery islands in the Mussel Ridge
channel. With his flint and steel he soon
had a fire ready to prepare his supper. He
skinned the birds, removing the skin and
feathers together, then split them in halves
and laid them on the coals, with a sprinkling

of salt. This with sea biscuit and a pot of tea composed his supper.

Under the boughs of a stately spruce tree that stood near high water mark, David made his bed. He cut boughs and covered them with the wherry sail, with his blanket for a spread, and turned the wherry over all, then turned in and slept as comfortable as if he lay in a bed of down.

The next morning when the sun was rising, David turned out and prepared his frugal, but wholesome breakfast. With buoyant spirits he sailed away, with a gentle westerly breeze blowing, continuing his course to the eastward. At the time the sun was at her meridian, he arrived among a cluster of islands of various sizes and descriptions. On one of these he landed on a pebbly beach, where there was an excellent boat harbor. He had particularly noticed this island when sailing in the old chebacco boat. It was a sight which he had seen before, but now on the island the scenery was fascinating. from all points of the compass. He walked around the island to see if he could find fresh water, and discovered a small purling stream, which led to a thick clump of evergreen trees. Bubbling there from a lime rock ledge was a delicious flow of water, clear as crystal. A few rods to the south of the spring there was a hummock with a ledge that formed a precipice facing south. The land surrounding the ledge was mostly covered with a young growth of balmy spruce and cedar trees, which concealed the ledge from view. It formed a complete barrier and shelter from the cold north winds, encircling the place from east to west. In this sylvan spot David built his cot and lived in rustic solitude.

Night was approaching, the beautiful July day was almost gone when David built a fire and prepared his supper. His gun and fishing line bountifully supplied his larder. His supper consisted of a black duck and a bloater mackerel cooked on the live coals. After supper he made his bed of boughs beneath the thick branches of a spruce tree, then turned the wherry over the boughs as on the previous night. Before turning in he replenished his fire and laid on the fuel so as to prevent its burning away too rapidly, and lay down on his bed of boughs, thinking and planning of his work tomorrow, until he went to sleep.

When he awoke the sun was up and shining and the birds were singing. With a sense of happiness, his thoughts reverted to the plans he had laid out for the day. Their accomplishment would afford him pleasure. He turned out, cooked and ate his breakfast, then commenced the hard but pleasant labor of building the chimney for his cabin, using the face of the ledge for the chimney back. He built two abutments out of flat rocks, making blue clay take the place of mortar, leaving a recess between the abutments which he arched over forming a fireplace, then extending the abutment connected to the top of the ledge. Then the chimney was complete. The chimney lasted good for years.

David's gravity and wisdom was beyond his years. He had educated himself by observation of nature, deriving his knowledge from a watchful attention to the whys and wherefores, and then drawing his own conclusions. Although ignorant in some respects of things that a school boy wonld be familiar with, nevertheless by a few well directed words he would confound a sage. David was no drone. He maintained his self-respect. He was no man's slave and no man's master, but preserved genuine independence, and was honestly willing to earn his bread. The few that knew him called him eccentric becaues he did his own thinking.

There was scarcely a river or stream in eastern Maine at that time but had a saw mill, with an abundance of white pine in the near vicinity. Of every log sawed there were left two or more slabs, which were set adrift as useless, this being the best way to get clear of them.

The next three days David in the wherry went beach combing among the archipelago or sea of islands, collecting these drift slabs, which he used to build his cabin. The frame of the cabin consisted of sills, plates, ridge plank and scantling, which he picked up or hewed out of slabs. The slabs for the walls he cut eight feet long, chipping the ends to a uniform thickness, then tree-nailed them to the sills and plates with the sawed side out. Then he covered them with sawed sides put together so as to break the joints, which made the walls double and tight. The roof was built in the same manner. The door was in the eastern end and opposite the chimney, with two windows, without glass, covered with sliding shutters. The floor was also made of slabs, sawed side up, and tree-nailed to the sleepers. His principal tools were an axe, saw, spike gimlet and jack-knife.

There is a kind of sedge grass that grows around marshes on the sea board which David gathered and dried. The pleasant odor of this grass lasts for years. He used a quantity of it for his bed, and the balmy perfume from the young spruce and cedar trees that thickly surrounded the cabin, afforded a most agreeable sensation. The cabin was not more than ten rods from the beach or boat landing, but entirely concealed. It was approached by a circuitous route back of the ledge, thickly spread with evergreen trees. The situation of the cabin was satifactory to David, for in his absence it would not be

DAVID ROBERTSON'S CABIN.

likely to be disturbed and would keep unwel-
come visitors away. David preferred seclusion and privacy. Nevertheless he would
occasionlly entertain a favored few.

The boat fishermen were often ashore on
the island digging clams for bait. With now
and then an excursion from the neighboring
islands, berrying in summer, he made a virtue
of necessity and kept his cabin concealed from
public view. By his industry and diligence,
working early and late, he moved into his
cabin the first of August, exchanging the
bough bed for the bunk of sweet scented
grass. The toil of the day had brought sweet
repose, and with his mind at ease and his
plans matured, he enjoyed the refreshing
slumber that comes of labor.

It had now become necessary for David to
leave the work that had afforded him so much
gratification. The pleasant days of August
and September were the halcyon days for

small boat fishing. With fish he could get all the necessaries of life, having no inclination for luxuries.

David left no opportunity neglected. With his habitual industry, during these months he caught fish more than enough for his frugal wants. Among the neighboring islands were owned several small vessels. In the fall of the year the fishermen would load one of the vessels for a western market with dried fish which were given to the captain in trust, to sell or exchange for their winter stores. A barter traffic was carried on in those times between merchant and fisherman, The merchant stipulated to pay one-half cash snd one-half in goods. David shipped his fish by the freighter, giving the captain a list of his wants including a few books to be added to his limited library, which comprised all told Bunyan's Pilgrim's Progress, Milton's Paradise Lost, his school books, almanac, Walker's

Dictionary and Bible. When resting from
labor David was educating himself. His
common sense and habits of reflection and
reasoning, in time brought about the result.

It had been previously agreed between
David and the captain of the freighter that if
he had an apportunity he would stop at the
island on his return and land his stores. It was
time for the fish freighter's return and David
was on the lookout. A signal gun informed
him of the arrival. With his wherry he soon
landed his stores. The settlement with the
captain was satisfactory. The returns sur-
passed his expectations. David had now
more than enough. Besides, a contented
mind is a continual feast, which is a self-evi-
dent truth that antedates the flood.

An educated stranger meeting David would
observe his gentle manner and would notice,
by his language, that he had obtained the
rudiments of a limited education, of course,

owing to his youth and the seclusion in which he lived.

During the few pleasant days of Indian summer David continued boat fishing, but when the cold, bleak winds of November made it solitary and comfortless, he found employment cutting wood for winter use, stowing it away in a hovel made of slabs. In the intervening time he had built a gunning float. The sea birds were abundant and with the float concealed with rock-weed, he could shoot more than he wanted. After plucking the feathers, the birds with the exception of black duck, were worthless. He used discretion, not shooting any more than he could pick. He found a ready market for the feathers he obtained from the sea birds, and they brought him ready money.

The black duck is by nature shy, suspicious and cautious, and considered by the rich and poor alike a luxury. Often he sat out on pleasure bent, on moon light nights, after black ducks, which afforded him pleasure and profit. Among these islands there were rivulets flowing into the sea, which the ducks frequent by night for fresh water. The black sea duck is by nature a night wanderer, wary and keen of scent; if approached from windward, he is off with a quack, and you have your pains for your trouble.

David built booths of boughs and would lie behind the blind concealed at times for for hours, but generally by this stratagem shot ducks enough to well pay for his mingled feelings of distress and delight. David now with all the comforts that rustic life affords, hidden from public view, the summer gone, the dreary days of stormy winter at hand, living alone in harmony with the laws of God, guided by reason, and envying no man, would not exchange his lot for the crown of a sovereign.

CHAPTER VIII

THE last days of January were extremely cold, the ice making on the shores so that the islands were enclosed with walls of ice. In February he went among the islands in the vicinity on the ice, with his gun and dog, after martins or minks, a kind of weasel which were found in great plenty on the rocky shore cliffs among the islands, the snow plainly showing their tracks. He would cross from island to island until the shades of night were beginning to fall, then with a back load of minks would hie his way home to his cabin. The pelts were a source of profit equivalent to money.

Roving amidst the islands in quest of game, it would sometimes happen that he would unexpectedly surprise and shoot a red fox. David's dog was a mongrel whose so-called instinct would surprise a naturalist, who will never admit that a dog is capable of thought. "Instinct" is not a satisfactory explanation of the sagacity and understanding of a trained dog, and it remains inexplicable, except upon the ground of some conscious intelligence. His dog was an excellent water retriever, rendering him invaluable when David shot wild fowl. She was delighted when allowed to bring or carry. When David went gunning after sea birds the instant the gun was discharged the dog was off after the fowl in the ice cold water in the coldest weather, leaving the dead birds in order to get the wounded first. They were halcyon days, for his labor was to him a pleasure.

The winter passed in tranquility and contentment, cruising or hunting on sunny days of winter, with his gun and dog, and elated with his successes, which he well merited by his thrift and industry. The evenings were invariably spent in the cabin, obtaining useful information.

When these islands were first settled the shore waters abounded in fish, mackerel, herring and menhaden being predominate. They were used for bait by the fishermen, in lieu of clams, when obtainable. Under the solar influence the ice embargo that had been on for two months was now disappearing. Signs of spring were making their appearance.

David was an inventive genius. He had never seen a fish weir, and all he knew about it was from a meagre discription given him by Skipper Davis when in the old chebacco boat. With a plan well matured, he now started to construct a fish weir, working early and late gathering materials, which were mostly obtained from the adjacent islands, then brought or towed in the wherry to the place where the weir was to be built. This work necessitated hard labor, yet the anticipation of the result made the labor a source of gratification.

From a point of land a sand spit extended from the shore forming an inlet or boat harbor. Here David built the weir, extending it into tide water below low water mark. His method of executing the work was simply by driving stakes and then interweaving alder brush, making a hedge, with a heart shaped trap at the outer end, covering the sides of the trap with a net made of marline. It was a long tedious job, he having to do the work alone.

He completed the weir the first of May. The boat fishermen had arrived, visiting David and offering suggestions. David listened with indifference, satisfied, in his own mind, they did not know what they were talking about. Arguing amongst themselves, one old fisherman said, " It's against common sense and reason to catch fish in a brush fence," and another replied: "So say I, if a fish went in that hole he'd swim out quicker than he went in, unless I am a fool." His prediction about the fish proved him a false prophet, as regards the fool, a true one, for David caught fish in the pound of the weir, in abundance. The weir being almost an original conception, proved a happy termination of his hopes and fears, the success of which greatly pleased him, but he was free from vanity and self-conceit. A barter trade was carried on between David and the fishermen, David furnishing the fresh bait in return for the cod fish, the traffic being satisfactory to both, likewise, remunerative to David.

When David had completed the weir his hopes were not realized at first. During the month of May he caught very few fish, with the exception of salmon, which he smoked and dried. Almost all fish are migratory.

The mackerel and menhaden did not make their appearance with June. These fish are very plentiful in the shore waters of Maine, with its 250 miles of ocean frontage, in a straight line from Kittery Point to Quoddy Head, including in its indentures of bays and rivers, a total of 2140 miles of sea coast.

The principal use the early settlers made of these fish was for bait to catch bottom fish. The three summer months were elysian days for David, who enjoyed the light labor of tending the pound of the weir, and curing the codfish which he received in lieu of the menhaden and mackerel caught in the weir. These fish were the equivalant of money.

By the world at large, money is reckoned as an important substitute for happiness, but it does not always bring it about. David, like the rest of the world, liked money, but would not sacrifice principle for it. There was no secret about David's making money: first, by well matured plans of labor which he accomplished; second, by industry, together with good common sense and genius combined; thirdly, he spent less money than he obtained, and could justly apply the old witticism: " Handsome is, as handsome does."

David now had plenty of spare time, and more company than was agreeable. The fishermen with their light and frivolous ways and speechifying, were not always congenial to him. Notwithstanding these defects, they were liberal, charitable and generous.

The summer passed away, and once more Old Boreas made his appearance with his icy blast, the signal for the fishermen to wend their way homeward. The fishermen all respected David for his estimable qualities, and many were the invitations he received to spend the winter with them in their humble cottages. David preferred the seclusion and privacy of his cabin with its enchanting visions, wherein he lived over again the scenes of the last winter, enjoying one of the greatest blessings of God to man, contentment.

It now became necessary for David to go in the wherry some distance, to see the captain of the fish freighter, to make arrangements with him to stop at his island, to take his fish for market. David set out at sunrise in the wherry, with a fair wind, arriving at the Captain's house at one o'clock. After making satisfactory arrangements, he then set out for home. The wind was ahead and blowing fresh. He kept under the lee of the islands as much as possible, keeping warm by rowing.

Night was fast approaching, when he landed on an island where there was a rustic farmhouse, built of logs and slabs. Hauling up the wherry out of the tide's way, he went to the house and knocked. A short, thick-set man came to the door and David explained to him the situation. With a cheer-ful invitation of "Come in, you are as welcome as the flowers of May," the old gentleman introduced him to his daughter and her husband. When supper was ready, he was cordially invited to "set by." The supper was abundant and plentiful. David being hungry, did the repast ample justice

There was a cheerful wood fire in the fire-place, serving to enliven and animate the inmates of the house. The evening was spent with sociable and animated conversa-tion, host and hostess dispensing a generous hospitality. The hospitality of the retired and primitive settlers of those islands was unlimited, and the stranger always found a cordial and kind reception.

The next morning, after an early breakfast, with a friendly parting, David was off for home. When he got within a mile or more of his island, his dog who had been left to watch, saw him with that keenness of vision with which she was endowed by nature. She swam off to meet him, expressing by actions, more than language can describe, her gladness.

The first thing done after getting home, was to put his merchandise in shape for shipment in the freighter. He stored and neatly packed the codfish and smoked salmon in convenient packages, also his pelts and feathers, with a dozen or more barrels of mackerel and herring. This work completed, he then carefully made out his list of goods. He could have the luxuries as well as the necessities of life, but he would have lived with frugality if he had had the exchequer or the revenue of England.

In due time, the freighter made the round trip. When the settlement was made, and he received his money and stores, the captain remarked to David, "You are high line among the fishermen this year." David had pride without vanity, and he received, with appreciation, the well merited compliment.

Captain Cook, master of the schooner Mary F., was prominent among the island towns. He had become somewhat famous for making quick trips, as a cord wood coaster. When on his passage home from Boston, he was overtaken by a heavy south-east gale of wind, in the Mussel Ridge channel. When he passed Owl's Head it was midnight. Under a double reefed foresail, he had to cross Penobscot Bay to Mark Island. His course was to leave Mark Island on the port hand close aboard, then through the thoroughfare into East Penobscot Bay. It was as dark as Egyptian midnight, the rain fell in torrents and the gale blew in tempestuous gusts. The schooner steered wild, owing to the heavy sea that was heaving in from the unbroken seas of the Atlantic. The wind was aft the beam.

The captain who was at the helm, not making proper allowance, the schooner run to the eastward of the course and struck on the rocks that lay to the eastward of Mark Island. The seas boarded the schooner in a terrific manner, staving the boats at the davits. The tide was making flood. The small chance of saving their lives, appalled the stoutest heart among them.

David was in his cabin to leeward of the wreck, when his dog began to act in a strange manner, howling and scratching at the door. David let the dog out and she ran to the shore, then back to the cabin, barking incessantly. David put on his oiled clothes and followed the dog to the shore. He launched the wherry and then rowed to windward, keeping under the shelter of the island, and crossed the thoroughfare by dint of hard rowing. With the aid of the dog, he succeeded in finding the wreck, and managed to get them on terra firma. The heavy south-east gales on the Maine coast are of short duration.

Next morning the wind was northwest and icy cold and very little was saved of the schooner. The succeeding months until February, David was hunting for minks or gunning for sea birds, with lucrative results. In February, owing to the severe cold weather, he stayed at home in the cabin, with a cheerful open fire that burned in the fireplace, ruddy and florid, dispensing comfort. He fully realized the contrast betwixt the warm cabin, and the cold, frigid weather outside. He was busily employed in the daytime, knitting nets or weaving ash baskets. The evening he spent with his books, which was his habitual custom, summer or winter, and so the days and nights alike passed felicitously.

The winter was severe, the longest continuation of sharp, cold weather ever known by the settlers. The bay was frozen to the outer islands. Horses with sleighs were crossing the bay until March. David's insular situation was now no protection, his island lying in a direct line of travel between the large island towns and the main land. He would often see teams hauling hay and goods, with now and then a traveller, who would stop and partake of David's hospitality.

David was so constituted by nature that he derived comfort from solitude and deep meditation. The days of winter passed quickly away. The ice was breaking up, drifting seaward. The welcome heralds of spring, the wild geese were on their passage northward. The jolly fishermen had come to their old haunts after early fish for home market. David now rebuilt the weir, which necessitated some hard labor, from dawn to sunset, but with the experience he had, besides his relish for work, it was soon completed.

CHAPTER IX

DAVID lived on the island for three years, with unalloyed happiness and peace and prosperity. The weir proved a successful undertaking. The *net* result of the fishing season appeared to be one that would leave him a competence, or at least a sufficiency.

In October, David packed his merchandise ready for market, and now anxiously looked for the fish freighter. A fishing schooner anchored near the beach. The captain directly came on shore, and appeared to be in a hurry, meeting David with a friendly salutation, with a pat on his shoulder, and a tongue as smooth as oil, using undue familiarity for a stranger, saying: "I have come after your freight, sent by Capt. W. Please use all the dispatch possible, as my business is urgent. I have stopped merely for your accommodation." Hurry was not a part of David's makeup. In his mind, he was entertaining suspicion of the captain, judging from appearances. The captain, now coaxing, now flattering, David listening. The captain now changed his tactics. " Well, I can't stay here all day. If you don't hurry up, I shall get under way and be off." David replied in two words. " You go," then walked off to the cabin.

For several days he was in a quandary, thinking what was to be done under the circumstances. He came to the conclusion that he would hire or charter a small fisherman and carry his own freight. There was a craft on an island in the near vicinity, that would suit his purpose. After making the necessary arrangements, and chartering the schooner, the freighter that was to take his fish arrived. David then related to the captain the incident of the vessel's coming after his freight. The captain had no knowledge of the transaction, nor could he, from David's description, recognize the vessel or the master. David canceled his obligation with the small schooner, and put his freight on board the freighter. The captain earnestly invited David to take the trip, so David decided to go, and went to Boston in the freighter.

David once more on board a fisherman, felt at home, ate his allowance, stood his watch, steered his trick, and helped make and take in sail, enjoying the familiar scenes with satisfaction. He had never been in a city, and when he arrived in Boston, somehow, it was not like what his fancy had painted. The confusion and noise were embarrassing to him.

The vessel lay at a wharf near Quincy Market. The October day was misty and chilly, when David went ashore for a stroll,

to look at modern Athens. He first visited
Quincy Market, where he had an opportunity
of using of all his five senses, gazing with interest and wonderment, as he slowly walked
through the market. Then he went to Fan-
euil Hall, and to Dock Square, crossing the
square to Washington Street, and gazing with
surprise as he leisurely walked. On turning
up West Street he came to the Common, and
loitered there for a time, until he called to
mind that it was time to go on board the
schooner. He started in the direction he had
come, but missed the turning. He walked
on, till he finally got back to the Common.
In this dilemma, he asked a boy the way to
the market. The boy replied: "Show you
the way, Mr. for ten cents." David said, "Go
on, I will give you ten cents when we get
there." "No, give me the money now, and I
will go with you sure." David, with suspicion, gave the boy ten cents. The young Arab

ran away with his thumb to his nose, wagging his fingers, and said " Verdant, you wait till I come back, and I'll show you the way to the market, sure."

An old gentleman who had witnessed this scene, understanding David's predicament, advised him to take a cab. With the gentleman's assistance, a cab was called, and an agreement made, to take David to Quincy Market for twenty-five cents. In less than five minutes, David was at the market. He passed the cabman a half dollar, expecting him to give him the change. The cabman said, " You are a gentleman," and was off before David had time to protest.

He was now in a fair way to get once more on board the vessel, walking hurriedly through the market, with only one idea in his head, to find the schooner. When he found the schooner, the welcome sight was something akin to the gladness of the mariner, when he sights land after being a long time at sea. When he got aboard, the jolly old skipper of the schooner, by dint of questioning, succeeded in getting the story out of David, and jokingly told the mate if David went ashore again, to tie a fish line to him, and make the end fast aboard.

David, if occasion required, could find his way across the Western Ocean, and the idea of his getting lost in the streets of Boston, caused no end of fun for the jolly skipper and his crew. Nevertheless, the next day David went ashore but paid attention to the course he was steering, keeping run of himself by dead reckoning and observation, with a sharp lookout for the lay of the land, as well as the bearings of Quincy Market, walking leisurely until he came to Cornhill. On the right hand side of the street he found an antiquarian book-store, and went in. A pleasant old gentleman was in attendance. This amenity at

once gave David assurance that the old gentleman could be trusted. He talked freely to
him, an unusual and rare thing, for him to do,
and voluntarily told him so much of his story
that the old gentleman became interested in
him.

David's object, when he entered the store,
was to get himself books, and he made known
his wants. The gentleman, without a mer-
cenary motive, helped David make an assort-
ment, and truly rendered him valuable assistance, showing that there is such a thing as
personal kindness among strangers in business
transactions, notwithstanding the maxim,
"There is no friendship in trade." Leaving
his books to be sent on board the schooner,
and taking a cordial leave of this gentleman
of the old school, David continued his ram-
bling, looking in the shop windows, or notic-
ing the passers by, speculating and theorizing,
and withal, somewhat excited by the superior-

ity of things open to his view. As he walked along feasting his eyes, he was accosted by an Israelite clothier with, "Come in my friend, I will sell you cheap, the best coat in Boston. I have got one coat that will fit you. The price is cheap at ten dollars. It is a genuine Liverpool pilot, and I will sell it to you for five dollars, mine friend. You come in and try that coat on." David tried to go on, when the Jew got him by the arm, to lead him into the shop. David thought the Jew was too familiar on short acquaintance, and gave him a shove that sent him head-long into his shop. When the Jew recovered his equlibrium, the epithet he applied to David was, "You Cape Cod, Down east, all along shore, son of a b——h."

David now started to go on board the schooner. He knew the bearings of Quincy Market, and course and distance would take him there. The general course he could define, but owing to the intricacy of the streets, with their labyrinthal windings, he was per- plexed and bothered. David came to a stand still on a corner, trying to decide what street to take, when he was greeted by an apparent- ly young woman, (who could hardly, with pro- priety, be termed a lady,) with a fond " How do you do, dear?" David's first impression was, that she had mistaken him for someone else, but when she invited him to treat her to a bottle of wine, David blushed with shame and confusion, and was off, when she said, with audacity, "You country lout, stop when you get there."

David, without further disturbance or trouble, arrived on board the schooner. The fish were sold, the freighter discharged, the stores were all on board, and the schooner ready for sea. The next morning, if the weather permitted, they would start the schooner for home. This being their last

Boston, the captain and his mate concluded to go to the National Theatre, and prevailed upon David to go with them. The dramatic performance of "The Forty Thieves," engaged David's attention, but it was contrary to his nature to be enthusiastically excited, and he was glad when the exhibition ended, as peace and quietness were more in conformity with his feelings than noise and tumult, Not so with the jolly skipper, whose guffaws and boisterous horse-laughs were hearty and repeated. These jolly old skippers that flourished fifty years ago, by their upright conduct and honest dealings commanded respect wherever known.

CHAPTER X

A LITTLE after sunrise, on the first day of November, with a moderate breeze they fiilled away for home. When the watch was set at eight o'clock that night, Cape Ann bore southwest, ten miles distant. In conformity with that class of vessels, the captain took her out, and the mate took her home, consequently, it was the mate's eight hours on deck. The night was dark, the stars obscure, the weather catching, so they decided to run the shore around.

The following morning, the weather was thick and hazy. They caught a glimpse of the land, which they called Seguin, before it shut down. They made their course good, for an hour longer, when it commenced snowing, and the storm had now come in earnest, with intense cold. The east wind howled and whistled through the rigging, while all hands were at work double-reefing the sails. They were now in a blinding snow storm and not sure of their position, amongst a large group of islands. The wind was blowing in tempestuous gusts, the cold increasing, and it was utterly impossible to turn to windward.

The skipper's countenance indexed his anxiety, but at length his troubled visage was lighted by a pleasing thought. He hailed David, saying, " Are you acquainted here? " David's laconic reply was "Yes." "Can you or will you, take her in?" "Yes." The confidence the skipper had in David when he said yes, amounted to more than a whole chapter of most men's talk. The anxiety that clouded the skipper's face, now vanished like dew before sunshine. The schooner was head reaching under close reefed main sail and reefed jib.

With the deep sea line, David got soundings after several casts of the lead. He then
slacked off the main-sheet and kept her off
with the wind on the quarter. The schooner
was now driving forward with rapidity, urged
on by the gale. The snow was falling thick
and fast, with heavy and angry gusts of wind
veering to the eastward. The sheet anchor
was all ready, with thirty fathoms of cable
overhauled. The schooner was going at a
fearful rate, for the rocky coast of Maine. If
by some mishap, now, David should make a
mistake, destruction would be inevitable.
Every man aboard was uneasy with a painful
sensation of danger, except David, who was
calm and composed, for he knew he was
going right. They could now hear the surf
breaking and roaring on the shore to leeward.

Soon after sunrise, the wind veered from
south to southeast. At eight o'clock, from
southeast to east. From where David got

OFF FOR MUSCONGUS.

night in soundings, his course for Muscongus, was north, northeast. David uttered the concise expression, "All right." Nothing could be seen, owing to the blinding snow storm, when suddenly, as if by magic, they were in smooth water.

He kept on for a mile or more, with occasionally a glimpse of the land to windward. It was now still and smooth, with hardly a ripple on the water, when they came to anchor. The exhilerating effect produced on these men, by the transition from imminent danger to absolute security, is beyond my pen to describe.

The roaring of the sea breaking on the out shores and rocky islands on the Maine coast in heavy weather, is called by the fishermen, "the rote." Coming in from sea, in thick weather, and hearing the rote, the fishermen can define their position and locate the rocks or islands by the rumbling noise of the sea breaking on the rocks. It was noon by the skipper's watch when they anchored off Muscongus. Their anxious care now gave place to cheerful and animated gladness.

The cook prepared an excellent dinner, to which all hands did ample justice. The tempestuous gale that raged at sea, brought them no anxiety, but they had sympathy for those who were unable to find a harbor of refuge.

David, now in a locality he knew so well, without loss of time, went ashore to visit Pemaquid. There he met with old acquaintances, and the usual greetings were exchanged, questions asked and answers returned. He learned that both the Commodore and Capt. Ben were laid at rest in the cemetery. He could get no information about Jack, as no one seemed to know or have any interest in him or his destiny. The old cottage had been torn down, with hardly a vestige left. The poplar tree that stood before

the old skipper's door, remained standing with
a grim and hideous appearance. The un-
welcome news caused gloomy thoughts, and
the melancholy scene where the cottage
stood, combined with the disagreeable day,
made David dejected. With spirits depressed,
he went on board. Devoted and faithful to
the memory of the place that had been his
home, he was displeased and disheartened
with his visit. The charms of imagination
were gone. Yet visions he retained, with
pleasant thoughts of his island home.

The next morning the wind had changed
to the northwest, an indication that the good
weather would not long continue. They
were under way and off for home at break of
day. With David for a pilot, they sailed
through the winding channels of these islands,
shortening miles of distance. On one of these
rocky islands to windward, they discovered
a wreck, apparently a schooner of about a

hundred tons, with a fisherman in the near vicinity, rendering what help was necessary. The schooner looked like, and probably was, the same that they saw off Seguin, before the snow tempest. They gave vent to many expressions of sympathy for the unfortunate schooner's condition, reflecting now that in all probability, they themselves, would have been in a similar situation, without David's assistance.

Without further incidents, the schooner arrived and anchored off David's island. In an hour's time, his freight was landed. David was full of gratitude for the kindness he had received, and the skipper also, was duly grateful to David for his assistance. Then with a hearty shake of the honest skipper's hand, they parted with kindly wishes for each other's welfare. The skipper went on board and sailed away.

David's dog, that had been left in care of a

neighbor, on the adjacent island, was at home
to meet him, greeting him with canine fondness. David treated her with endearment.
She had manifested her affection for him by
her actions, as plainly as words could describe
her joy.

The chilly November day was almost gone,
when David built a roaring fire in the open
fireplace in the cabin. Nothing had been
disturbed. He prepared his frugal supper,
eating it with all the relish of youth and
health. Then he sat in his easy chair before
the genial fire, in cheerful meditation, living
over again the scenes of the last two weeks.
He realised the truth and beauty of the grand
old song, "Home, Sweet Home."

CHAPTER XI

ON one of the clusters of islands that was near to David's lived a family of more refinement than the ordinary settlers. They were Massachusetts born and bred, meeting with adverse fortunes while living there. Hearing novel tales of the natural advantages of these islands on the Maine coast, they decided to settle there. Mr. Lane was a smart and stirring man, past middle age. Both he and his wife, were people of education. They claimed to be descended from Scotch nobility, having a record of the family genealogy.

The family were hardy, strong and healthy, and well adapted for a pioneer's life in a new country. His family of two boys and five girls, came with him when he took up the land, and secured his claim as a settler. Working with an enthusiastic zeal, he cleared the land and built his log-cabin, and eventually received the reward that honest labor is sure to bring.

When Mr. Lane came he brought his library, which caused his neighbors to look on him with respect, and he was always treated by them, with a kind of reverance, as long as he lived. Mr. Lane entertained a favorable opinion of David, frequently inviting him to his house, and nothing would have pleased him more, than to have had David for a son-in-law. David was popular. His fame had spread amongst all the islands, far and near, on the Maine coast. More than one excursion was planned by the fishermen's girls, to go berrying on his island, (to fish for David.)

The girls of Mr. Lane were skillful at rowing a wherry, and often came alone for berries. David always gave them a wide berth, for he was a bashful fellow. After various unsuccessful attempts to engage David in conversation, the lively, rosy-cheeked one, the girls called Mary, at last let her temper get the best of her, and called David "a freckled gawky," and went home in the sulks. Several days passed, before Mr. Lane's girls went to the island.

When Mary got over her ill-humor, these merry girls went back on the island after berries. They were busily engaged picking berries, and did not heed the approach of a tempest. A flash of lightning, followed by a heavy clap of thunder, sent the girls running and screaming, to David's cabin for shelter. What stratagem and wiles failed to do, accident accomplished for the girls, viz.; they got into David's cabin.

Now they determined to see if they could not get something out of him besides monosylables. The whole five of them began to ply him with questions, all talking at once. David was nearly distracted. He was no match for these girls who outnumbered him, five to one. More than that, his retreat was cut off by a sentinel on guard at the door, and escape was impossible. While the shower continued, his cabin was under petticoat authority. Mary particularly noticed David's collection of books. While looking them over, she mentaly planned a scheme to trap him, after his cruise to Boston, in November. The scheme, she put into execution.

Mary knew that it was his usual practice to spend his evenings reading or studying. She took from her father's library the first volume of Cooper's Deer Slayer, and got her brother to devise an errand to David's and leave the book on his table. Her brother did as she directed, and after doing his necessary errand, went home. David found the book on the table, with Mary's name on the blank leaf, wondering, without suspecting, how it came there.

After supper, sitting in his easy chair before his cosy fire, he began to read Mary's book. He soon became interested, and as he read on, his interest increased. Nothing short of an earthquake would have taken his attention now from the book. He finished reading it that night, and the next day went to Mr. Lane's house for the second volume. David bit the insiduous hook that Mary was angling with. Mary saw him coming and was flushed with the success of her scheme.

Mr. Lane and his wife received David with a hearty welcome. It was the first time he had been there. Mr. Lane said he and his wife were both honored to receeve a visit from him, and he would be pleased to see him in the future. When David was ready for home the malapert Mary passed him the book, neatly done up and tied with a string, with a mischievous twinkle in her eye. She said to herself "O, he will come again, he has got the first volume of the Scottish Chiefs in the bundle."

David, like other men, had a sensitive feeling for a pretty girl. He had now discovered that Mary had beautiful eyes, dimpled cheeks and alluring ways, and was brimming over with fun. Is it any wonder that he bit at the bait? He went home with the picture of Mary and her ways, impressed on his mind. The calm and sedate David was in love, as men in all ages, have been, and will continue to be as long as time shall last.

Mary was right in her prediction and David now went often to Mr. Lane's house. David was fascinated by her ways and beauty, but somehow, Mary, with all her wiles could not make him talk to the purpose. Nevertheless, his actions implied what no words expressed.

David now was a constant visitor at Mr. Lane's house, acknowledged and received as a suitor for Mary, and well appreciated and valued by Mr. Lane and his wife.

Mary had made all the advances that maiden modesty would permit, but still, David made no proposal. She was determined not to be the old maid of the family. David was equally determined to act consistently. He had not solved the problem to his satisfacttion. With precipitation on her part, and procrastination on his, the lovers were at cross-purposes.

When David went home, Mary's sisters would quiz her about him, wanting to know what he said. Mary's answer was "None of your business. The freckled clod-pated dolt didn't say anything." Mary's tongue was remarkably expressive, and her temper was not always pacific.

The winters David spent on the island,

were remarkable for their long continuance of cold weather. The present winter was no exception. In February, a strong bridge of ice formed, so that his neighbors could go and come at pleasure. The consequence was, that David had to entertain more company than he wished. He entertained them with hospitality, but invariably, his guests did the talking, but enjoyed their visit none the less, for fishermen would rather hear themselves talk, when they have someone to listen.

The days came and went. David remained at home. His solitude which he loved so well, was disturbed by too much company, now that he was mentally trying to analyze his feelings regarding Mary, whom he credited with many virtues. Since their tiff he had been disposed to blame himself. David's symptoms plainly indicated his disease, which, even a quack doctor could diagnose, namely, a bad attack of love-sickness. David was not using the proper remedy, common sense. It was true of him, as of sage and fool alike, that when common-sense and a pretty girl are weighed in the balances, common sense generally goes for naught.

For two weeks, David had not seen Mr. Lane or his family. When one day, Mary's brother made his appearance with a billet-doux for him, from Mary, stating there was to be a merry-making that night, and that she wished him to come and go with her. Her sweetly expressed and neatly written letter was answered with the brief, but comprehensive words, " I will come."

These merry-makings were not to David's liking, but somehow, when Mary said "go," David went. David, dressed in his best, and went after Mary; she received him at the door, and put her little white hand in his great, rough paw, then arched her neck so as to put her handsome face near enough for him to kiss her. The brown freckles on his face turned red. He then did the best he could.

David had ice creepers on his feet. When they started to go, it was necessary for her to take his arm, for the ice was slippery. They trudged merrily along, Mary's tongue running uninterruptedly, except by David's monosyllables, as happy now as the birds that sing in the spring time, arriving at the old fisherman's house, filled with ecstacy.

All the young people for miles around, were there or coming. At that time, the fishermen's houses were all built alike. They had a large brick chimney in the centre with fire-places in each of the three rooms, which were petitioned off with matched pine boards, unpainted but kept scrupulously clean by the good housewife and her girls. The fishermen's houses were not only built, but furnished alike. The furniture consisted of high-backed, basket-bottomed chairs together with a homemade settee, an escritoire, which they considered indispensable, a clock with a mahogany case reaching from the floor to the ceiling, usually standing in the front room, and a pine table, also made at home. A pole hung from the ceiling and a gun stood in the corner. The fire-place in the kitchen, was of extensive dimensions, conspicuous with the iron crane, pot hooks and trammels. Such were their homes. They were noted for honesty and plain dealings, were without poverty or riches, and stood on an absolute equality.

On this occasion, at the old fisherman's house, there was a roaring fire in all the fire-places. The old fisherman and his wife were in the front room, each in their respective corners by the fire. The old man sat in his easy chair, smoking, the good housewife, in her rocking chair, with her knitting work, while the boys and girls stood ready to welcome each new arrival. When David arrived he, by particular request of the old fisherman, was ushered into the front room and seated beside the old man, who had a great regard for him. To use his own words, he "set store" by him.

It was a pleasure to the old man ostensibly to entertain David, but in reality, himself, by telling his stories that David knew as well as he did, having heard them many times before. David thought the old man's mental faculties failing, especially his memory. While listening to a story about capturing a privateer in the war of 1812, with ballast stones, a dozen or more girls rushed in for David to pay a forfeit. David, attacked front and rear, squirmed unsuccessfully. The old fisherman sang out, "Gone by the board. Taken by surprise. Rake 'em fore and aft, David!" But he had to lower his colors and surrender. Tucker, himself, would have had to strike against such unequal odds.

The old fisherman said "it was not a fair fight. Ten to one, they were rigged all right, and just out of the dock, coppered, scraped and painted from royal-truck to scupper-hole, but no good in heavy weather, and the way they fight is a disgrace to the continental navy.

With few exceptions, the settlers on these islands, in days of yore, were sailors. In the Revolution and the war of 1812, many of them served in the navy or on board a privateer, and after the war, they became fishermen. As long as they lived, their language was sprinkled with nautical phrases. The language of their descendants, now scattered over the world, no matter what their business, is also tinctured with marine phraseology. The ancient maxim still holds true, namely: "As the old cock crows, so the young one learns."

Among the party, there was a foppish young sailor, dressed in a new suit, his head greased with pomatum, his white handkerchief scented with cologne, on his hands, a pair of gloves to cover up the stains of tar, and making more trivial talk than was becoming.

The old fisherman with his fiddle, struck up the musical notes of "The Flowers of Edinburgh," the signal for the contra dance. The young sailor went after Mary, who was not going to be left because David could not dance. She kept up a kind of flirtation with the coxcomb, so marked, that it attracted notice.

Later on, David began to grow jealous and envious of the fop, and felt as if he would like to wring his neck. The old fisherman, like the rest, noticed the proceedings, and not liking Mary to act as she did, watched a chance to say a few words to her. "Mary, I don't want to hinder you from enjoying yourself,

but that sailor fellow doesn't amount to much.
I knew him and his folks. His grandfather
piloted the English into Castine, in the Revo-
lutionery War. My advice is: Don't swap
David for the like of him. I know 'em
both. David's got an honest hand and a heart
as pure as gold. The like of him is not found
every day." Mary sullenly pouted, and made
him no answer, but when out of his hearing
said, "I wish the old fool would mind his
business."

David had excellent self-command, yet his
countenance was strongly expressive of his
feelings. He was sitting by himself, in reverie,
when he was startled by a pat on his shoulder
from the old fisherman, with the brief and
wise council, "You never mind, David, she
isn't worth the powder." Mary's brothers
were there. David said to them, "I am
going home. I wish you would look after
Mary."

When Mary found that David had gone home without a word to her, her maidenly goodness and principle caused a reaction of her feelings. The capricious Mary, now gave the cold shoulder to the dandy sailor, and went home with her brothers, showing ill humor.

David went home thoughtful and pained at heart. His feelings were not of anger towards Mary, but he grieved inwardly, making no outward show except a deep sigh that would escape him now and then. Lucid burned the fire in his cabin. His dog fawned but received no caresses. He could not read or sleep, but simply sat by the fire in serious contemplation, trying to reason the thing out to his satisfaction. His final conclusion was live or die, he was done with Mary. Alas, the day! It was a long time before he found the tranquility of mind that was necessary for his happiness. He went about his usual vocations, thoughtfully and with a placid calm, yet with a touch of sadness. He truly loved the capricious Mary.

It was not his nature to seek fools for company, or drown his troubles in strong drink. Although his mind was made up, still, visions of her comely face, continually haunted him. The visionary castles that had offered him so much pleasure to build, he now realized, were a fool's paradise. He had never solicited or courted company, but now he avoided all comers. In the evening, he sat staring at the blaze that sent forth a bright and sparkling light, prevading the cabin, allowing his thoughts to wander whither they would. If he took up a book to try to direct his mind from his trouble, after reading pages, he had but a vague idea of the sense of the author's words. David so laid his love of Mary to heart that he lived the life of a recluse, now, in thought and deed, with unceasing thoughts of Mary. He could not obliterate her from his mind. The demon, jealousy, was inflaming him, and jealousy is akin to love, and as long as jealousy lasts, love remains.

March had come and gone, and it was springtime with the mild west wind in contention with old Boreas with his stormy, cold and snowy north winds blustering yet, and loath to die. The ospry, or fish hawks, had come to re-build their nest on the old pine tree that stood in plain sight of his cabin, where season after season they hatched and reared their young. The red-breasted robin and chirping sparrow, which he so gladly welcomed the spring before, now, he scarcely noticed. The fishermen, as usual, dug their clams, wondering where David was, and why he did not build his weir.

David was taken unawares, one day, by Mary's brother who handed him a letter. David knew it was from Mary. The superscription was in her hand writing. He stood musing for a time, without a word, with the letter unopened, until Mary's brother made some remark to attract his attention. David then wrote on the unopened letter, the single word "Farewell," and passed it back to Mary's brother, and walked away to live again, forlorn and desolate, amongst these wild and desert islands.

The next eccentric thing that David did, was to load his wherry and a bateau with his belongings. He fastened up his cabin and barricaded the door, then wrote on the cabin, the concise word "gone." But where, for how long, was a puzzling question to the fishermen. To avoid the inquisitiveness and curiosity of the fishermen, David sailed away before sunrise in the wherry, towing the bateau. His destination was a solitary island, remote from the haunts of men, where he could enjoy solitude to his heart's content. It was not far distant from an inhabited island on the north, but east, west and south, there was nothing except the boundless Atlantic ocean. The island was covered with ever-green trees, with a shingle beach that made an excellent boat-landing, and there was an abundant supply of fresh water.

Arriving at the romantic and rugged isle, before noonday, he at once commenced to build his camp in a sheltered nook near the spring and close to the boat landing. David's inventive genius was of a high order, as I have said before. His primitive ideas and his originality were not often excelled. He built a comfortable and cosy camp with an old sail, and covered it with spruce bows that made it warm when the weather was cold, yet cool and shady in a hot summer day. The building of the camp, occupied both his body and mind, and diverted his attention from the affliction that had sorely troubled him, The

days spent building the camp, brought him
what money cannot buy, viz: a placid and
peaceful contentment. At night, on a bed of
balmy boughs, he slept the undisturbed sleep
of health and tired nature.

It was Saturday when he completed the
camp. Like most of the ancient fishermen,
he was observant of the Sabbath, though not
to the extent of the rigid doctrinal Puritans
of those days, but his worship was regulated
by moral sense. He was a scrupulous
searcher of the sacred scriptures and a firm
believer in their mandates. The Sabbath he
devoted to rest and tranquility, meditating on
the precepts that God's Word enjoins. During the retired life which he led, he devoted
to himself diligent study, and he was learned
and versed in the Holy Writings. His previous trouble now gave place to quiet and
blissful contentment, and David once more
enjoyed life.

His time was spent in the forenoon, fishing, and generally before the sun was at the meridian, he had caught a wherry load of fish. It was his habitual practice to neglect nothing, however trifling, and never put off till tomorrow what ought to be done today. His observance of this simple rule was the principal and essential cause of his prosperity in his undertaking. By strictly adhering to this practice, he succeeded where others failed. When he came in from fishing, he prepared and ate his dinner with a relish that the healthful occupation of boat fishing is certain to guarantee, with an appetite and digestion that an epicure would prize above rubies.

Contrary to the usual habits of fishermen, David, in a neat and tidy manner, would put everything in its proper place. He fully realized that he had all the time there was, and always used an hour to do an hour's labor. His life now passed like the flowing of a deep and gentle river. The transitory spring days came and went pleasantly, notwithstanding his regular routine of labor. His work was not fatiguing or irksome, and was without hurry or turmoil.

His solitary life was uninterrupted except by a singular character, known by fishermen, as Uncle Simon, who for years had made his appearance during the summer months, in same locality, in his small schooner, living aboard, but fishing in his wherry and salting the fish down in the schooner's hold. They often fished within hailing distance of each other, and after a time, the best of feelings existed between them. Uncle Simon's taciturnity was fully equal to David's, and his company, therefore was congenial.

David was only twenty, and Uncle Simon three score and eight, but nevertheless, there was a great similarity in their characters. The essential difference was, that Uncle

Simon thought, that owing to his age and experience, he had a right to be tenacious of his own opinion and judgment, versed and tried by the experience of so many years fishing. Uncle Simon would occasionly manifest this trait of his character. David would readily acquiesce, never contradicting or gainsaying his opinion, and willing that Uncle Simon should enjoy his singular notions. Accordingly, he regarded David with fondness. But David caught more fish, which had a tendency to take the conceit out of Uncle Simon.

It is natural for those who are interested in the history of David, to desire to know the meaning of words that have been frequently used in these pages. The dialect employed, was in use more than half a .century ago, among the fishermen on the Maine coast, and at the present time, these words have not become wholly obsolete, Reference Dictionaries for the phraseology will be of little assistance, for if the words can be found at all, they will often be defined in a sense not used by the fishermen.

CHAPTER XII

IN the month of September, between the fortieth and fiftieth degree of latitude in the north Atlantic Ocean, foggy weather is not usual. A fog mull or mist interspersed with showers for ten days during the month rendered the weather disagreeable. The fish had struck off, and David with Uncle Simon went about two miles southerly of the island to catch some. A glim (a word used by sailors and fishermen) discovered the form of a ship laying by, with her topsails to the mast and her ensign in the main rigging. By invitation of the Captain, David went on board, and the first question the former asked was, "Who is President of the United States?" David replied, "Martin Van Burin." Is he a Whig or a Democrat" asked the Captain.

David answered "a democrat." "Thank God the country is safe" ejaculated the Captain wtih patriotic zeal.

The appearance of this Captain indicated his character, which was ostentatious and over-bearing. Regarding David as an inferior and unimportant man, he addressed him in a pretentious manner as follows: "I am from Canton, loaded with tea and silk, and bound for Boston. I have not taken an observation of the sun for ten days. We got soundings during the morning watch, and found rocky bottom, but there are no such soundings laid down on the charts." David replied, "You are on the eastern coast of Maine." "I know a d——d sight better than that" rejoined the Captain, "As course and distance have carried me all over the world time and time again, and don't you undertake to tell me my ship is on the coast of Maine." David made no reply, but hauled up his boat to get in, when the Captain now grew less arrogant, asked how Cape Ann bore and at what distance. Not liking to have his veracity questioned, David answered, "Course and distance will carry you there if you know how to run them."

The Captain now became compliant and invited David into the cabin. A Mercator chart was spread out upon the table. With marked condescension in his manner he said, "If I am on the Maine coast how did I get there?" David replied, "If you navigated by that chart it is no wonder that you are off your course, as all the meridians are straight lines perpendicular to the equator and greatly exaggerate your course, and besides you have not made enough allowance for the Gulf Stream."

Nothing could exceed the surprise of the Captain to hear this explanation from so young a man, whom he had regarded of such little account and to find him so well versed in nautical science. Now, being satisfied of his position, and with his conceit well ended, he filled the ship away on her course south-west half west about one hundred miles for Cape Ann, having first courteously presented David with a small chest of China tea.

Time wore on and a month had passed away. The weather grew boisterous and stormy. Uncle Simon was preparing to re-turn home when an unexpected event hap-pened. He saw something conspicuous float-ing at thewindward of the island, in which he called David's attention. The latter went to the promontory, and with a spyglass dis-covered it to be a dead whale. Uncle Simon wanted to make fast to his tail, but David said, "We can never tow him in this way." Uncle Simon was very susceptible of anger when contradicted. He stood up in the wherry waving his arms and said, "If you undertake to tow him head first you will have to take the Atlantic Ocean along with him, for his mouth is big enough to swallow the boat." Not convinced, however, David let Uncle Simon have his way and made fast to its tail with a fishing rode*. The wind was fair and they both worked vigorously at the oars for over an hour when Uncle Simon became discouraged. "Now," said David, "Let us try him head first." "We might as well try to tow Agamenticus*," said Uncle Simon in reply, but reluctantly gave his consent. David then made the rode fast to the whale as near the head as possible. The whale floated on his side, his head with the big mouth that had perplexed and harassed Uncle Simon was under water. Whether it was open or shut was a quandary.

The wind was fresh to the southward, with the sail on the wherry, while David and

---

*Rode, a rope used by fishermen to anchor their boats when fishing and made fast to the anchor or a stone called by them a killock.

*Agamenticus is conspicuous and a noted land mark by the fishermen. It has been seen on ship board when forty miles or more distant.

Uncle Simon bent their backs to the oars strong and powerful. They soon had the satisfaction of seeing the whale following in the wake of the wherry. After a hard pull they grounded the whale near David's camp on the shingle beach. Obstinately, with a firm adherance to his own opinion, Uncle Simon said, "We could have never got him ashore if the wind had not breezed up." David made no reply. It was almost night; after making the whale secure, and then eating their supper, turned in to obtain the needed rest that tired nature demanded, fully realizing hard labor would be in order for the next ten days.

The following morning an assembly of fishermen had congregated, expressing their opinion how many barrels of oil the whale would make. It became necessary for Uncle Simon and David to employ help to try out the whale. A kettle was obtained from a neighboring island, and now hard work and a plenty of it for a week or more, resulting in forty barrels of oil—a piece of good fortune Uncle Simon called a God-send.

When the oil was ready for shipment they fortunately found a freighter and shipped the oil and their fish for a western market, Uncle Simon going in the freighter as supercargo as far as his interest and David's was concerned.

The weather being chilly and the nights cold, he could no longer keep comfortable in the camp. He now put all his belongings on board the pinkey, and sailed early next morning for his island home. The cabin if it had not been molested would afford comfort and warmth. He would from choice have spent the winter on this desolate isle, solitary without company, if his camp would have protected him from the inclemency of the weather.

He arrived at his island home about mid-day. The cabin had not been disturbed. Before night he had everything in well-regulated order, making a fire and then getting his supper, which on this occasion consisted of a bowl of gruel for the reason he had contracted a severe cold while trying out the whale oil. With this exception the cabin afforded him a refreshment of spirits with a feeling of rest and quiet, a reverse from the bustle and tumult of the last fortnight, which had not been agreeable to him.

Before turning in for the night he brewed a pot of thoroughwort or boneset tea, which he drank down, but it did him no good. The next morning his cold was worse. He kept about for three or four days, when a continuous fever set in. He now, a part of the time was delirous, yet in his rational or lucid intervales of reason he realized his condition. He sent his dog with a note tied around her neck to Mr. Lane. The dog had been trained to

fetch and carry, and understood what was
wanted and speedily executed the errand.
Mr. Lane with his daughter Mary were soon
at the cabin. Mr. Lane quick to understand
the real state of affairs said, " Mary you stay
here while I and the boys go to the main for
the doctor. We shall probably be back early
tomorrow morning if by chance we find the
doctor at home."

Mary, born with good sense and not wanting confidence, immediately went to work to
make him gruel and herb tea and putting
things in order generally. David laid in a
kind of stupor, apparently insensible, murmuring with a low articulate voice, unintelligibly.
She tried to get him to swallow some gruel,
and after a time she succeeded by urgent im-
portunity, by using kind and gentle words.
Mary, quick to contrive and inventive to
manage, made ready use of her intellectual
abilities, and before the doctor arrived the next

morning, had everything clean, and the cabin looked comfortable and cosey.

In due time Mr. Lane with the doctor arrived at the cabin, and without delay he examined David and shook his head and said, "I ought to have been called sooner. David is a very sick man, his fever is now seated and I cannot break it up and it will have its course." He then said to Mary, "You will have to be the doctor, all will depend on you, keep up his strength with nourishing food that he can digest." Then leaving an opiate and a tonic with instructions for their use he was ready for home.

The west wind that had been blowing a fresh breeze in the forenoon, at noon was a brisk gale. The boat they had crossed the bay in was not competent to go back. The doctor said he must go if it were possible, as he had a patient he must see that was dangerously sick.

There lived on the large island to the leaward, Captain H———, who was the owner of a whale boat. Mr. Lane went to see him in his boat and explained to the Captain the condition of affairs. The old captain called for volunteers to man the whale boat, and he soon had six stout and vigorous young fishermen ready to cross the bay any time when the old captain said go. They were off in a hurry with the old captain in charge, dressed in oil-cloth, standing up steering with an oar, while the six young fishermen bent their backs to the oars with a will, jovial with mirth and gaiety, although for the time living in two elements, air and water. Getting the doctor on board well covered up in tar-pauling, they were off for the main shore. The doctor was popular with sailors and was their principal physician for more than thirty years.

Mary's vigilance and watchful care and honest devotion to David's wellfare, obeying the doctor to the letter with a strict constancy to duty, under her careful nursing he at last began to recover strength. Her inconveniences were numerous, but she overcame all obstacles with ingenuity, being quick to see the means that suited the ends.

During his sickness Uncle Simon returned to adjust and settle the account of David's shipment with bills and papers for vouchers. David was delirious and much against Uncle Simon's will, he was obliged to settle with Mary. She had already taken a dislike to him the for reason of his obstinate and perverse ways. Uncle Simon was honest and Mary was acute of mind and penetrating to look after David's interests. Uncle Simon's hasty temper caused him to show Mary disrespect because he thought she did not verify his statements. Mary, yielding to the dictates of prudence, using discretion and keeping her tongue under submission until Uncle Simon had paid her the money, then let it run rendering him no thanks for his favors. Uncle Simon bade her a grouty farewell, then went on board his pinkey and sailed for home. As soon as he was gone she muttered, "Well that old man is destitute of good sense, but I got out of him all the money that belonged to David."

It was a pleasant still day as is sometimes seen before winter comes in earnest, and valued more for their scarcity, when David's faculty of reason returned to him. Lying in his berth, trying to make out what it all meant, he was free from aches or pains as his fever had now burned out. He lay in his berth in a quiet and calm meditation. The weeks that had passed were obviously unintelligible to him. Mary was sitting in a rocking chair sewing, the fire in the fire-place burning clearly and brisk. The sun was shining through the dwarft spruces and cedar thickets, throwing a mellow light on the cabin floor. The stand stood near the head of his berth covered with a cloth as white as snow, and upon it a small tray containing a wine glass and two or three phials and a few lemons. The floor was as clean as sand could make it, and everything was orderly and scrupulously neat. A bunch of chrysanthemums in a vase adorned a shelf, making a striking contrast between their beauty and the rugged and uneven walls of the cabin. His dog during his sickness had lain on a rug in front of his berth, now sat looking him in the face slowly wagging her tail, apparently realizing that her master had recovered consciousness, manifesting it by a low bark. The bark of the dog with a quickness of apprehension which Mary inherited innately, hastily brought her to his bedside.

Although he looked poor and emaciated, yet his eyes brightened and his visage lighted up with pleasant smiles when he perceived it was Mary. He was about to speak when

Mary put her white hand to his mouth and said, "Don't you talk David." She directly got him some broth, which she always had ready, made from sea birds, liberally supplied with rice. He received it with the same pleasant smile, drinking a cupful with an apparent relish.

Some of Mr. Lane's family relieved Mary nights. She saw her brother coming, and ran out to meet him to tell him the glad tidings. She had done her duty and no mother could have done more for her son. The happiness which she now felt sprung from enjoyment, a benificent disposition to do good. The antiquated maxim has grown old and out of use, but remains true nevertheless: "Virtue brings its own reward."

If there is a destiny that shapes our ends, no man constitutes his own history. He can only palliate and conceal it. Every new day brought renewed strength to David. Mary's

watchful care never relaxed as long as he was
an invalid. Her care for him during his dis-
ordered indisposition undermined and weak-
ened her affection in a measure. The familiarity which was brought about as his nurse,
was partially the cause of the reaction of her
feelings. Every day he improved and every
day she grew less anxious yet cautious, giving
heed as she ought, to her maiden modesty;
still her heart was full of a mixed sensation of
love and sympathy. She possessed all the
good qualities, also one or two more. It was
evident now that Mary was no love-sick maiden pining and wasting away.

David now was fast recovering his health
and strength, and had become so enamored
with Mary that he made love to her with a
full intent and purpose as honest and as honorable as was ever offered to the shrine of a
goddess.

David like other men was not entirely destitute of conceit, yet he had no haughty or proud opinion of himself. All the gratitude he felt for her, and his old love revived this love, for Mary was genuine, chaste, and faithful. Whether he was now a sage or fool or six of one and a half a dozen of the other, the sequel of David's adventures or history show.

Mary with all her good qualities was yet capricious in mind and temper. After being relieved that night and going home she sat up late in meditation. The result was she would not marry David, and assigned to himself the reasons: first, he was carrot-headed, and freckled as homely as a brush fence; second, he would not talk, and was no company for anybody; third, he was a hermit, and had rather live in a camp than a house; fourth, he is jealous pated. She kept on enumerating his failings without giving him any credit for his moral goodness, and with a burst of ill humor went to bed in the tantrums.

The next morning when her brother came home from David's and was ready to ferry her across, which had been his usual practice, Mary said, "O he's well enough, I shan't go over till after dinner, then I will go and cook him some victuals. He is as ravenous as a wolf. If he could get all he wants to eat he would breed a famine." David spent the forenoon watching for Mary, with an uneasiness of mind, having a craving appetite, and at most high noon he began to cook some dinner for himself.

There had lately been introduced among the island homes the tin kitchen and the tin baker, a decided improvement over the Dutch oven and the spider. Knowing their value by their use at home, Mary had sent and bought them. David considered them an innovation, so he baked his bread on the spider and suspended the fowl from the mantle before the fire, and put the potatoes in the Dutch oven to cook his dinner his usual way. While the dinner was in progress Mary arrived at the cabin, and with an emphatic utterance she said, " What are you doing? why don't you use the baker and kitchen?" David made her no reply. Mary talking to herself, "Well there is no sense in him, using that old Dutch oven and spider." Then with a flirt, quickly put the fowl in the kitchen, the bread in the baker, and soon had dinner ready.

If she had turned the cabin upside down he would have entered no protest. He had a chronic love-sickness and was suffering a relapse of his former bad state, pressing his suit with fondness and affection for Mary to be his wife, in his homely way. Mary not knowing her own mind would neither acquiesce, nor refuse compliance with his request.

Her actions on this occasion perplexed and harassed him. Still she adhered to them with conservative tenacity which nearly drove David distracted. After Mary went home, she used the privilege that lovers are allowed, the enjoyment of soliloquy. "Well, I suppose I have got to have the fool, but he has got to get off that island and build or buy a house fit to live in where I can see somebody and live like other folks. Besides he has got to get a cook stove. Then I will heave the old Dutch oven and skillet out of doors, and he will have to sleep on a bed-stead instead of a box like a lunatic." She kept on until she had exhausted all her volubility.

David now once more with gun and dog betook himself to his own diversions of pleasure and profit, and went hunting after minks when there had been a light fall of snow, at other times after ducks and sea birds, with his usual success. In pleasant days in his wherry he rowed for miles among these unfrequented woody islands, as in days of yore, charmed or fascinated still.

When he returned home at night, after preparing and eating his supper, instead of sitting before his fire with his book, he now in-

variably went to Mr. Lane's home and spent
the evening with his family, but Mary was the
only attraction for him there. He went, in
hopes to get a chance to press his suit, but
went home night after night disappointed.
Mary neither by word or actions, alluded to
the subject nor allowed him any opportunity,
nevertheless David had patience and perseverance both, to overcome the difficulty. If
by luck or chance an opportunity offered him
to say a word of endearment to her, (using a
fisherman's phrase) she would snub him with
a round turn *standing*. The fact was Mary
had two strings to her bow.

ONE afternoon David was sitting in his cabin thinking and contemplating and somewhat dejected withal, caused by his blind love for Mary, never doubting but she was worthy and amiable, when his dog barked with her ears pricked up. It was a stranger that had come, or his dog would not have barked. A knock at the door also indicated the presence of some one. A strange man now stepped into the cabin. "Are you David Robertson?" he inquired with a broad Scotch accent. "Yes," was the concise answer of David. "It a gang long row from the main land, I will have to introduce myself and business. I am a Scotchman, born and bred in Scotland. My name is Holiday, and my vocation is a fisherman, and its many the trap I have set and weire I have made on the Solway, Clide and Lorn Firth, and many

the muckle fish I caught in the lochs of bonnie Scotland. I have heard of you and your
weir and I have come to see what can be
done here. The winter lies heavy on the glen
in Scotland. The fish are growing scarce, so
I have come to seek my fortune in the new
country, where report says a poor man would
do well."

A social evening was spent by Mr. Holiday.
He appeared to be an enthusiastic, talkative
man and David thought he knew what he
was talking about. David listened with interest to hear him narrate particulars and descriptions of taking fish in Scotland. When
it was time to turn in, Mr. Holiday said, "I
would like to have you go with me tomorrow
and I will liberally pay for your trouble."
David answered, "Tomorrow is the Sabbath.
(which he always regarded with veneration).
My observations of nature and the Holy Book
convinces me of an invisible power: A
Supreme Being in whom I believe. There is

a command in the Book to regulate our moral
conduct: viz, Remember the Sabbath day and
keep it holy." The Scotchman, stung by this
unexpected rebuke, with pathos bowed his
head, remarked, "I beg your pardon: I dinna
ken, Gude preserve us, tomorrow was Sunday," using his Scotch dialect when animated
or excited.

David in this respect was only following
the example of many of the fishermen in early
times. Tithing men were chosen by the
island towns for the special purpose of having the Sabbath observed.

David then said to Mr. Holiday, " If agreeable to you, stop with me. On Monday I will
go with you, and show you some localities
where the outlook is good to build weirs.
On Monday a storm of snow and wind obliged
them to stay snug in the cabin. Towards
night it stopped snowing, when David sug-
gested to Mr. Holiday to go with him to visit
at Mr. Lane's, which Mr. Holiday readily

agreed to. The distance being short, they soon arrived at Mr. Lane's house. David introduced Mr. Holiday where they received a cordial and hearty welcome. Mr. Holiday was agreeably entertained by Mr. Lane. Few could please or divert their guests as well as Mr. Lane, while none could do it better.

Mr. Holiday and Mr. Lane discussed business, politics and religion with mutual satisfaction. David said little, as usual, thinking and drawing his own conclusions, with now and then a modest and diffident look at Mary. Mr. Holiday was observant and noticed the sheep's eyes David cast at Mary and understood what it meant. He possibly in his palmy days had been in the same boat.

When they were returning to the cabin Mr. Holiday broke out with a mixture of Scotch and Gælic, "On, ey! David, she has a blue een, with dimple cheeks and as bonnie a lassie as the sun ever sheen on, and Scotch blood in her veins, I canna be mistaken, David, ye will

noo see the like of her, except in the Glens of
Scotland. What a dower she will bring ye
too. A house full of bairns that will keep ye
name green for generations."

Three or four still cold days succeeded the
snow storm. David and Mr. Holiday in the
wherry, went cruising among the group of
islands that thickly studded the eastern coast
of Maine, to find a suitable locality to build
the weirs. The set of the tide has to be
taken into consideration. After mature
thought and deliberation, Mr. Holiday concluded to build several on the western end of
a large island, so as to get the benefit of both
the east and west bays of the Penobscot. Mr.
Holiday proposed to David to join in partner-
ship together, but David respectfully refused,
and remarked, "Your ways are not like mine,
nevertheless I will render you all the assistance I can." The disappointed Scotchman
said, "Well, well, you are a pleasant companion and an arch lad, but somewhat scatter-

brained, and not mindful of what is best for you. 'You get your whak, and get na mair'." * That Dulcinea with the blue eyes and the fair hair has turned your head, and you have gone "daft," allowing his quick temper, so easily vexed to get the advantage, with the next breath begging David's pardon.

Mr. Lane was a fine specimen of an old school gentleman now growing old with a gradual failing of health. His oldest son whom he had not seen for three years, who had been to sea, on foreign voyages had come home to see his parents. He commanded a fine ship and possesed a certain dignity of manner, besides the reputation of being one of the most capable ship masters belonging to Maine. " A good son maketh a glad father."—a trite expression, and I know of no better one.

When his son stepped into the house a tear of joy was in the old gentleman's eye. With filial love he said, " I have a good mind to kiss

---

*Meaning you get your portion of food and get no more.

you my son." "Well," he rejoined, "kiss me father," his mother manifesting her joy by clasping his hand, with her fond eyes of blue beaming with admiration for her noble son. Mary and her mother were all that were home. The other girls lived in Massachusetts and were married.

The cooking of delicate niceties for him by Mrs. Lane and Mary was no irksome task, but an enjoyable pleasure. Go where you will, roam where you may, there are no victuals so savory or relishing so well as the cooking of those old time mothers. He said, " Mother dear, I have the best the world affords aboard the ship, but nothing ever was so good and palatable as your cooking."

He staid with his parents at home only three days when absolute necessity compelled him to go. A destiny unutterable by decree or fate seemed now to follow Mr. Lane. His youngest son, whom he expected to be the support of his old age now wills to leave and go to sea. His father, mother and brother did all they could to discourage him but of no avail. The next morning they saw their son, the captain with his brother depart. Sad and lonely now was the old home with no children left but Mary. Misfortune never comes alone. Another calamity followed hard. His wife was taken sick and confined to the bed. It seemed to him there was nothing left but hope, and even that he was making a poor use of. David now in turn staid with Mr. Lane, looking after his interest, knowing what ought to be done, and doing more than was absolutely necessary, distinguishing himself more than ever by his profound taciturnity.

Mr. Lane took it for granted and looked on David as his subsequent son-in-law, and to serve and care for him in his old age. The confidence he placed in David was unlimited and he merited and earned it by his faithful fidelity. Reference has been made that order was a leading trading trait in David's char-

after. Before a week had elapsed the general appearance of the house and surroundings looked more like a gentleman's residence than a rustic farm house.

To a gentleman of Mr. Lane's refined intellectual discernment this personal quality of David's was in accordance with Mr. Lane's will and pleasure. He looked on David as a benign benefactor.

CHAPTER XIV.

MRS. LANE, poor woman, was wasting away with the fearful and terrible disease, consumption,* at times flattered by delusive hopes, at other times giving up in despair. An aunt of the Lane family, hale and hearty, who was a lady of uncertain age, but eventually ten and forty (for it is one of the hardest things to remember an old maiden lady's age) with her nephew of twenty, who had come to live with Mr. Lane at his request, the aunt to do the housework, the nephew to do the farm work.

Mary's invalid mother now needed all the care she could bestow. Mary did all for her

---

*The Pulmonic Consumption was the scourge that laid waste and made lonliness and solitude in many of the primitive fishermen's homes on the coast of Maine, and caused no doubt by privations and hardships they were obliged to endure. The disease was the cause of great anxiety owing to its deceitful nature. The patients themselves were often hopeful while their friends knew that dissolution was inevitable.

mother that could be done with aptitude and tenderness, never swerving from her duty or manifesting any signs of ill humor. No mother had a more affectionate daughter.

Previous allusion has been made to David's character in the following respect, he had a natural impulse to prepare and have ready what was necessary without making disturbance or trouble.

Miss Mary, seeing how good David was, her heart swelled and yearned towards him, but her secret meaning and real intention was to let him go if her scheme did not miscarry.

The vernal March once more began to thaw the ice on the rocky island shores breaking it up into cakes, while the prevalent north-west winds drove them southward. The willow was now putting forth its buds tipped with soft, feathery down. The wild untamable sea-gulls light on the shore nearer than is their wont to the fisherman's cottage, while now and then is seen the aquatic birds of passage returning north. These signs are the welcome heralds of spring that make glad the hearts of the humble fishermen.

David now concluded to build a weir extending across the passage from the island to Mr. Lane's. It would be superior and of greater extent than his original, and so constructed as to take the fish coming and going through the passage. William, Mr. Lane's nephew and hired man helped David build the weir. It was of primitive construction and not in conformity with Mr. Holiday's ideas. Mr. Holiday was at work in the vicinity and paid David a visit one day, voluntarily giving him counsel and information in relation to building the weir, but David built the weir in accordance with his own judgment. David and William labored diligently and the progress corresponded to their labor. The last day of March the weir was complete. Mr. Holiday at that time had four weirs in progress and none complete. Help was scarce and hard to procure. David now made his word good and helped Mr. Holiday execute and complete his weirs, yet still living and making his home at Mr. Lane's.

David, during the cloudy and hazy month of April, assisted Mr. Holiday to complete his weirs, fulfilling his promise. William proved to be a faithful and trusty man and had an abundance of time after his farm work was done, to look ofter David's weirs.

The first of the migrating fish that make their appearance are salmon and alewives. The salmon were smoked for market. The alewives that were caught were mostly sold to the fishermen. Mr. Holiday now considered himself under an obligation to David, and well he might, for he had rendered Mr. Holiday valuable service by hard and tiresome labor. Nevertheless the Scotchman was conceited in his notions, and self-willed. The information he had voluntarily imparted to David, he considered as equivalent in part for David's labor.

Mr. Holiday built the weirs in imitation, in part, after the kind in use in Scotland, with hooks, traps and pounds, which David thought a part were superfluous at least. If David made a suggestion to save labor Mr. Holiday would answer in reply, "Ay, ay, my bonnie laddie, you wait a bit," with unbounded self confidence. David received an inadequate compensation for his services. In the meantime the nebulous month of April gave place to May, the dreary winter that brought solitude and gloom on the lonely isle, now gave place to balmy spring.

Mrs. Lane yet with hopeful expectations as the days went by became weaker, until at last she was reconciled to her fate with composure. She had discharged all her duties to her husband, her children and the world, to the best of her ability. Early one beautiful May morning, a short time after sunrise her spirit returned to her Creator. Upon her placid features was a pure and peaceful look as if she were asleep, taking her rest. So quiet and tranquil was the departure of her soul to God that her husband and Mary at her bedside hardly knew when the separation took place. Her memory has been kept green by her children and her children's children. Truly the memory of the just is blest, for the reason that she lived her life in conformity to the laws of God.

They laid her to rest in the field near a maple tree, when the western descending sun shines on a tree, it shades her lonely grave. Half a century has passed and gone. The golden-rod and clover blending with the grass, bloom over her grave, and gongs of birds on the branches of the maple still sing her requiem.

Mr. Lane regarded his wife with excessive fondness. Unhappy and pitiable he sat in his arm-chair with his head bowed down on his breast day after day, apparently in a hopeless state of despondency. David tried to encourage and animate him with but poor success. Now and then he would give utterance to his thoughts with the brief words, " My poor wife," followed by a sigh.

One day Mr. Lane said to David, " Do you think I will ever see my wife again in the habitation of God? I have not obeyed the laws of God as I ought," David, instead of answering his question, handed him the Bible and his spectacles, calling his attention to the frequent allusions pertaining to the question in the Holy Scriptures, mentioning chapter and verse, allowing Mr. Lane to find them. After reading the passages with intellectual admittance of their precepts, Mr. Lane found the question answered which he had asked David. David then remarked, " I hold it is deviating from God's law to murmur, and not be reconciled to your wife's death." Mr. Lane with penitence and contrition said, " For the rest of my life I will sacredly try to live in obedience to God's divine laws."

Mr. Lane, by divine grace, was restored to a sound state of mind, his disquieting condition now giving place to a more cheerful manner. In the meantime things seemingly began to improve. David when not employed in tending the weir, devoted himself to the useful purpose of agriculture, improving on the mode of tillage that had usually been practiced by Mr. Lane and his neighbors, and obtained better results, lightening the labor by exercising his power of doing the work with ability. With his good common sense he reigned supreme over Mr. Lane's dominion.

As the spring passed away, his management of the farm showed wisdom and discretion; but always acting in conjunction with Mr. Lane, who on his part was perfectly willing for David to do as he had a mind to, because he saw that he had hold at the right end.

David still continued very much in love with Mary, and unaware he had a rival.

After a decent interval of mourning had elapsed, he once more pressed his suit with courage, in his homely manner. Mary in reply was petulant, and called him a stupid monomaniac, but David did not seem to mind it, with a strong adherance to the trite maxim, " A faint heart never won a fair lady." Patience and perseverance were strong traits of his character. As long as he did not see any cause of jealousy, she might taunt him to her heart's content. He never lost his patience, and would bear her expressions with the air of a martyr. He did not understand Mary at all.

The Jack-a-dandy sailor when in foreign parts had been secretly corresponding with Mary; and when at home, on several occasions paid her a visit, but by chance or design, presumingly on Mary's part, he had never met David,

These proceedings of Mary's were a source of annoyance, weighty and troublesome to

Mr. Lane, but he lived in hopes that Mary would come to her senses.

The sailor was not without friends in Mr. Lane's house. Even the spinster sister of Mr. Lane had become a proselyte of Mary's sailor. After listening to his marvelous Munchausen tales of mountains of sugar, rivers of rum and mermaids innumerable, all daughters of Amphritite, and wife of old Neptune, who was father to the whole of them.

Mary's sailor was at home wherever he happened to be. On every opportunity he made love to Mary with obstinacy that outweighed reason, being proficient in vows of the same kind that men have made and not many have kept, since the time that Adam was numbered with transgressors.

David in a happy ignorance how matters were proceeding was early to bed and early to rise, with the prospect of a bountiful harvest in the near future for his honest labor. The weir was a success with lucrative results, even better than he anticipated. The sequel proved that his agricultural labor as well as his fishing, left him with abundance and ample store, owing to hard work combined with good sense and a set purpose. More than all, whatever he did he did well.

The sailor-dandy's subtile flattery and obsequious manner was not without effect on Mary. The stronger the flattery the greater the influence.

His good looks, smooth tongue and fluency of cheap talk suited the fancy of the capricious Mary. She had her misgivings, nevertheless, but would do as she had a mind to. Her father might prate or preach, but she would lie in the bed she had made, and it was none of his business or anybody's else. Mary in vindication of herself could not help making comparisons in the sailor's favor.

When the ripe wheat and golden corn were harvested there was abundance and to spare, and the heart of David was gladdened by the sight. And when prosperity had reached the climax, unbeknown to David, Mary went off with the dandy sailor, with nothing to his credit excepting what he had on his back.

Poor Mr. Lane! The children he had reared so carefully and in whom he had tried so hard to inculcate the moral duties of religion and virtue with faithful instructions in the ways of wisdom, had now all forsaken their home to seek what they will never find, the content and happiness of their childhood days.

Another source of trouble to poor Mr. Lane was what David would do when he told him that Mary was gone. He was well aware that David would receive the bad tidings hard, but was in hopes he could comfort and cheer him. Mr. Lane dreaded to tell David of Mary's inconstancy, but he knew it was his duty and swallowed the bitter pill. After deliberate reflection he made known to David the sad story.

David was confounded with astonishment,
and dumb with silence. What were his
thoughts no one ever knew, for he never gave
them utterance. That night he went back to
his cabin followed by his faithful dog. The
next day Mr. Lane told William to go over
to see David and carry a message, consisting
of sympathetic and friendly expressions
united with affection, for him to come back.
William went but could not find David.
The cabin door was fastened and all was still
as the silence of mid-night. William went
back home no better off than when he came.

The days and weeks went on, and the
frosty nights of October were followed by
chilly November, and yet Mr. Lane had not
seen or heard from David.

On a pleasant Indian summer day a fish
freighter anchored off Mr. Lane's fish house
when, Captain W. went on shore. Lo, David
was with him! Mr. Lane seized David by
the hand, and holding it, with a pleasing

countenance and eyes beaming with gladness.

Then and there with hands joined, stood two honest men, the noblest work of God, one old and venerable, the other young and respectful, and both marked and characterized by candor and justice.

Mr. Lane with words that excite tender emotion said to David "Don't never forsake me again. I have a mental perception that old age advances rapidly, My white head, impaired vision, and trembling hand are sure signs of the near approach of the grim tyrant that has been a terror so many years. I have now lost my dread, and now I am revived and comforted by the promises in the Holy Book, and am ready to welcome the harbinger with hope and courage."

Time seemed to make no difference with the jolly old skipper. He now entered his protest, saying, "I have been trying to persuade David to go this trip with us. I am already indebted to him for saving my schooner, and probably my life. It is now late in the season, and with David on board I would feel relieved. In bad weather I can depend on him. I shall be back in ten or twelve days if God wills." Of course David could do as he pleased but as yet he had not said a word.

Mr. Lane yielded to the skipper's earnest entreaty, and David went once more on board as a fisherman, after a promise to Mr. Lane that he would come back and report. As many hands make light work they soon boated the fish and surplus of the farm productions on board the freighter.

Mr. Holiday was on board with his fish and the freighter was deep as a loaded sand-barge. The jocose merriment of the fishermen with the talkative Scotchman was good medicine for David, and he had to take it in large doses, nauseous as it was to him and it did him good, because he could not think on account of their frivolous talk.

It had been a calm day, what the fishermen call a weather breeder. At night a gentle mild air breezed up to the morth-east, and this being a fair wind they were off and away for Boston the next morning at eight o'clock. Monhegan was beaft the beam, the wind north-east and increasing. "What do you think? She will be up with Cape Ann before six o'clock at this rate?" The mate replied, "I think we had better let her go until noon, then if it comes on too tough or shuts down thick David can make a harbor long as as we can show a rag of canvas." All went well, and early next morning they arrived in Boston under double reefed sails. For a week after a heavy north-east gale raged at sea.

NOTE   The heavy gales commence to the leeward and it is often the case that moderate north-east winds off the coast of Maine will be blowing a brisk gale off Cape Hatteras. Hence a vessel sailing south-west with a north-east wind is sailing into the gale.

Historical records make allusions to this remarkable gale. Navigation suffered on the Maine coast severely and it was the heaviest gale within the memory of the old fishermen. This remarkable N. E. gale happened in December, A. D. 1839. Of sixty sail that anchored in Cape Ann harbor for shelter fifty-five were wrecked.

CHAPTER XV

DAVID'S rustic manner had improved. He did not attract notice as on his former visit, and no longer gazed with astonishment like an awkward country bumpkin. The young Arabs no longer artfully practiced their tricks nor made him a butt of ridicule. Even the Courtesans and Jews let him pass without remarks or observation.

In wandering around the docks David's close attention was drawn to a small schooner with a sign on her foremast, "For Sale," and he carefully looked her over. She was well adapted for a fisherman, with good accommodations, good sails and well fitted generally, and as a whole pleased his fancy.

The wharfinger who had the care of her, remarked to David, "You can buy her cheap, the owner has no use for her. He has to pay

wharfage and also me for taking care of her."
David asked the wharfinger the price, and in
reply the wharfinger answered: "Three hundred dollars, and that is less than half what
she is worth." David replied, "I will give two
hundred dollars, if I can be guaranteed her
bottom is in good condition."

The wharfinger with a show of anger,
mixed with an apparent disgust said, "If he
gives her away it will be to some of his friends
not to you. If that is your best offer you
will never own the boat." He asked David's
name and address, then with the usual compli-
ments each went his way. The next day the
owner of the schooner accepted David's offer,
and David thus became the owner of the
schooner, Rover.

There was a poor apology for a man who
had been hanging around the skipper of the
fisherman for two or three days without
money or decent clothes, soliciting a passage
in the freighter. He told a deplorable story

of ruin caused by the demon rum saying, "I do not want to stay here as I am so passionately addicted to drinking spirituous liquors that I have become a habitual drunkard. My only chance left is to go where I cannot obtain it." His honest confession caused David to look on the poor inebriate with compassion. In a pleasing manner David said to him, "Will you go with me?" "Yes," he replied, and then went with David where his schooner lay. While on the way David purchased his outfits to last him home, and when they were on board the schooner David said to the man, "Are you willing to go with me in the schooner?" "Yes, where you go I will go gladly if you will have me."

David with trusty confidence in the man, handed him a ten dollar note to go and get some necessary clothing for himself. The man with genuine surprise and with a tear in his eye, said, "There is not another man in Boston who would trust me with money and

THE ROVER.

you with your kind heart would not if you
knew me as well as I know myself." He
went out and was back in a short time with a
pair of cheap boots, a pair of trousers and a
woolen shirt. He gave David back the residue of the money with the remark, "This is
the first time for ten years when I was sober,
with money in my pocket that I passed a bar-
room without a drink of liquor."

With the stores aboard they dropped the
Rover off the point of flats and let her swing
to her anchors. David now asked the man
his name. In reply he said, "You may call
me Smith, but that is not my name, for I am
ashamed to tell an honest man my name."
"Do you object to stop aboard alone and look
after the schooner, Smith?" "No, for a long
time I have slept on a brick floor in an engine
room. I am glad of an opportunity to sleep
in a berth." David then told Smith he could
set him ashore, and said, "Tomorrow is the

Sabbath, you come to the slip at Long Wharf in the dingy after breakfast."

When David landed he directly went on board the freighter where he was hailed by the jolly skipper with, "Well, I am glad to see you, I could not think for the life of me what had become of you. There are no land sharks hereabouts that know enough to get you foul. When you went off you had old Hard Up in tow. What did you do with him? He is no good only for eel bait." David without reply to the skipper's oratory inquired if he was ready to go home. "Yes," rejoined the skipper, all ready these two days, waiting for the weather to clear up and the sea to smooth down. "What do you think, David, shall we have a clear day tomorrow?" "It is the Lord's day tomorrow, skipper," David replied, "and I hope you will wait until Monday. I am not going home with you in the freighter." "*What,*" exclaimed the skipper, struck hard aback. "What will

THE ROMANTIC STORY OF DAVID ROBERTSON. 217

I say to Mr. Lane? I, myself heard you tell
Mr. Lane that you would come back with us."

At this, mate, cook, Scotchman and all
chimed in with the skipper with their protest,
"David falsify his word," they muttered.
"That is preposterous." David said, "I shall
try not to break my word with Mr. Lane. I
told him when I left I would come back and
report." The skipper knew by experience
that it would be of no use to pump David, so
the enigma remained unsolved when all
turned in for the night.

The Sunday morning that followed was
clear, calm and cold. After breakfast David
went to Long Wharf. His man was there
waiting, looking miserable with his bloated
face. His blood-shot eyes and trembling
hands quivering involuntarily like an aspen
leaf, all betokening his misery. Leaving the
dingy in care of the man that had charge of
the slip, David bade Smith go with him.
Smith would have walked behind David like

a menial, but David insisted on his walking
by his side. David was devoting an honest
zeal in a good cause.

They leisurely walked on towards the north
end of the city, and soon arrived in the locality that had been the haunts of Smith for a
decade of years. Here was where the old
topers congregated then as well as now, and
none was more familiarly known there than
Smith. As they passed on they were saluted
by a sot who had arrived beyond the bounds of
decency, "I say 'Hardup,' where did you pick
up that psalm-singing hypocrite? Will he
stand treat if I go along with him?" The
sweet notes of the chime bells were agreeable melody in David's ears, and in his imagination they seemed to say, "Peace on earth,
good will to men," and impressed him with
awe and veneration to God and his laws. "I
am going to Father Taylor's Church, and
want you to go with me Smith, and show me
where the church is, and go with me." Smith

said, "Father Taylor has often-times tried to get me to go to meeting, but I would not go. I will go with you, but I should think you would be ashamed to go to church with me." When David and Smith went into the church Father Taylor exclaimed,

"Hallelujah! Here is the old Misery in port with the old ship of Zion's pilot aboard. The Misery has been sailing under counterfeit colors for ten years, and now wants overhauling from royal truck to scupper-hole, and her bottom calked and coppered before she is sea-worthy. She ain't fit to sail in company with the old Zion, who always lands her cargo safe. Brother Sailor, don't be afraid to ship in the old Zion. She will carry you safe through all your troubles and tribulations. She is staunch and sound as a pump bolt. When driven by storms and lashed by tempests she will land you at last in a snug harbor, with all those that sail by her chart and steer by her compass. Now brother sailor let me persuade and advise you. In your watch below read in your Bible the fifty-first psalm. When you are beset by storms, when the tempestuous gales rage. and the nights are dark and drear, and you have to stand to the deck in the cold rain, remember the mandates that God enjoined. If by chance you escape a watery grave, or are buried in the ocean, while life lasts ever remember God's ordinance and keep his command. If you comply with God's precepts you are certain to arrive at a peaceful haven at last, where the poor storm-beaten sailor will obtain eternal rest."

The dejected appearance of poor Smith was pitiable indeed. The tears fell from his eyes, and many an eye was moist that heard

the venerable man. Father Taylor*, with his
arms extended, then pronounced a heartfelt
benediction and dismissed his congregation of
men that follow the sea. Mid the cold and
cheerless hours of night when the poor de-
luded sailor has to stand his watch of eight
hours on deck, the sympathetic expressions of
Father Taylor would often comfort him with
the hope of a future reward. David and
Smith left the church together and leisurely
walked side by side without exchange of sentiment, each in silent communion with his
own thoughts, to the place where they had
left the dingy and separated, Smith to go on
board the Rover while David went back on
board the freighter.

The heavy north-east gale that had raged·

---

*Rev. Edward T. Taylor, born in 1793, died 1871. He was a Bethel
minister in Boston from 1830 until his death. "Father Taylor," as
he was called mingled nautical terms and figures in his discourses,
and by his wit, pathos and magnetism controlled the minds and
wrought upon the feelings of his hearers in a remarkable degree.

at sea for the week past had at last become
pacific, but as yet the weather remained un-
settled. Early Monday morning the skipper
filled away, leaving David on the pier, who
cast off his fasts. With a blithesome manner
unusual to him he wished the skipper a pleasant passage. The good old skipper was
seriously troubled to leave David behind, but
could give no satisfactory reason or motive
for David's actions. The Scotchman, who
had his oar in on all occasions said, "That is
a short story and soon told. David will never
come back, and many a good man besides
David has gone wrong when jilted by a trifling young woman." The skipper with a
burst of passion at the insinuation of the
Scotchman said, "When David goes wrong
you will see the dead ducks flying over the
dry lochs in Scotland."

A short time intervened before David was
underway and following in the wake of the
freighter. There were light airs and calms

with passing clouds for twenty-four hours after leaving Boston. The next morning they were off the Isle of Shoales. The light winds commenced to breeze up with heavy clouds rolling up in the south-east and a bright glim low down in the western horizon. The sea had gradually changed color from a blue to a gray black. These signs David well knew meant that a snow storm was brewing and concluded to make a harbor before night if possible.

David, who had kept astern of the freighter by intention and for a purpose, now properly trimmed his sails and was soon along side of the freighter to leaward with Smith at the helm, while David kept himself from being seen by those on board the freighter.

The old skipper on board the freighter hailed Smith with his vociferous voice, "Schooner ahoy!" Smith answering dictated by David, "Hallo! Where you bound?" Smith replied, "Going to try to make a harbor in Portland. If it shuts down to snow before we get there we shall go in to Wood Island."

David let the Rover range ahead of the freighter a mile or more, and then slacked off his fore sheet so the old skipper could keep in company.

At twelve o'clock the wind increased, and both schooners had all the wind they wanted. David double reefed the mainsail. The old skipper carried his three lower sails for an hour longer to try to keep up with David, when he had to douse, and put two reefs in one, fore and aft. David now took in his foresail so as to keep in company. At three o'clock it began to snow but David had the bearings of Cape Elizabeth when it shut down, now with the good harbor of Portland under their lea where they safely anchored before dark.

On that memorable stormy, dismal 'December night tradition and history both say the snow fell between sunset and sunrise eighteen inches. The next night the wind came off to the west-north-west. The weather was clear, and the quicksilver in the thermometer stood at zero when David got under way for home, leaving the skipper to come when he got ready.

David came to anchor off Mr. Lane's house a little after sunrise the next morning. The freighter rounded to close aboard David's schooner late in the afternoon, and with evident surprise the skipper said, "That is our company-keeper. I wonder what she is a doing here? As I am a sinner there is 'Old Hardup,' if I am in my senses. The skipper with astonishment went ashore where he was met by Mr. Lane and David, with extended hands to greet him. David remarked with a twinkle in his eye, "I came a little ahead of you skipper to report."

The skipper after discharging his freight took leave of Mr. Lane and David with expressions of sincere affection and good will which was returned by them, with a hearty

shake of hands, left them and sailed away to
his eastern home.

NOTE. The fishermen a half a century ago would greet each other
with a cordial and warm reception when they met, and with a corresponding feeling of regret when they parted. The world is morally
better because these men lived and flourished. As like begets like,
and as their descendants are scattered over a wide domain and receive
innate their traits of character from their progenitors, good results
came thereof.

Between the years of 1835 to 1845 so entirely engrossed were the
inhabitants of these islands and their environs in shipbuilding that
they neglected their agriculture and fishing interests. In most every
creek from Bangor to Thomaston were being built coasters, brigs and
ships, and to a limited extent from Quoddy to Kittery. These vessels were extensively manned by fishermen, so while navigation and
shipbuilding flourished, agriculture and fishing were abandoned by the
young people. Fisherman and sailor are synomymous terms in a
measure, for it was not of rare occurance that the young skipper of a
fisherman at middle age became a ship master, while the deep water
young sailor who had merited the distinction of a ship master in the
regular order of progression would be of but little use and no orna-
ment on board a fisherman.

CHAPTER XVI

MR. LANE'S oldest son had become a man of influence. While David had been absent he paid his father a visit and persuaded him to move off the island. The Captain (his son) was the owner of a large estate situated where all the necessaries of life could easily be obtained. A vessel was hourly expected to transport him and his chattels. The greatest drawback was the transportation of his hay and getting his flocks and herds on board the vessel. David offered a suggestion for Mr. Lane's consideration, which was to have the stock wintered on the island. "It would save moving the hay, and I will see they are well cared for." "That will never do David," replied Mr. Lane, "I want you to go with me."

The Captain was mindful of the strong attachment his father had for David. With ample means at his command, and having no wife to draw or divide his affections they all centered in his family, particularly his father. It was a gratification to the son to please his father, no matter at what cost.* The inducement the Captain offered David to go with his father was that David should be a joint heir with his brother and sisters at his death.

David respectfully declined. His singular way was that of but a small part of mankind, and besides he had a little secret which he had kept well protected. He did not like the old maiden sister of Mr. Lane's.

After a time the vessel arrived that was to convey Mr. Lane and his people with their movables. Mr. Lane had decided to leave the stock in David's care. He felt downcast and dejected to leave the place that had been

---

*The Captain died wealthy and his money established the basis of one of the institutions of education in New England.

his home for years. The venerable man who was once strong-minded manifested signs of dotage when he shook hands with David. He then said, "If our tenancy of life continues may we perchance meet again and finally meet in the celestial dwelling where dis-uniting can never exist," and then with heartfelt sorrow went his way.

David would have desired to spend the winter in his cabin in privacy. He had an ingenious scheme in contemplation, which was that he could take fish in nets and do away with the hard labor which the building of weirs necessitated. He enjoyed himself at all times best alone, especially when he was mentally at work on some project. Hence the least company he had the better he was pleased.

An old and somewhat eccentric fisherman with Mr. Holiday for a companion would now and then pay a visit to David in pleasant days, but in bad weather he was well rid of them for the reason that it was too much like work to row the wherry to and from his island. When there they could sit around his open fire telling stories alternately; the Scotchman relating the wonderful heroic deeds of renown of the Highland Chieftain in Scotland, while the fisherman's stories related to Maine localities, each in turn listening with pretended credulity. As a general thing the stories they told were without merit or worth, nevertheless it was a pleasing satisfaction to each of them to hear themselves talk.

When the old fisherman's turn was in order he said to the Scotchman, "Did you ever hear the story of the twin brothers, Mike and Jim?" "No, but I have heard—" "Belay that Mr. Holiday, it's my turn you know, Ha,—I shall have to tell it to you. You are the only man on the Maine coast that has'nt heard it.

"Jim and Mike were twin brothers who were owners of a sloop and found employment carrying cord wood to Boston. They were captain, cook and all hands in turn. And as merry fellows as ever lived, and often-times played their jokes on one another. If Mike played a joke on Jim, he would bear it with a facetious merriment, and then bide his time and pay Mike the principal and interest.

"They were on the passage home from Boston in the old sloop on a pleasant summer night. It was Mike's eight hours on deck. At twelve o'clock he called Jim. Mike went below and turned in, and in five minutes was fast asleep. Jim went below and set the watch ahead to four o'clock and sung out: 'Four o'clock brother Mike, it's your watch on deck.' Mike turned out and said, 'Brother Jim, I never was so sleepy in my life.' but went on deck and took the tiller, while Jim turned in for another snooze.

"At five o'clock there were no signs of daylight, six o'clock and still no daylight. Mike was awe-stricken with terror and went down and sung out to Jim, 'Turn out, Brother Jim, there's going to be another dark day.' "*

The Rover was hauled up in a sheltered nook or cove almost hidden from view by stately trees, where she lay secure against the turbulent and tempestuous storms that prevail in winter on the coast of Maine. Smith, who intended to winter in the cuddy of the schooner now became a tenant of Mr. Lane's and lived in his house subservient to David, and took care of the barn and found employ-

---

*The remarkable dark day which astonished and amazed the settlers, was a theme for conversation among the fishermen for many years and used by them in a chronological manner to mark events as before or after the dark day.

ment cutting wood for a dollar a cord, the money being paid him every Saturday night. The monotony of his secluded life was hardly congenial, but he willingly bore the brunt, and was proud of himself to be a man again.

He was having a hard fight against the demon rum, which had brought the curse, disgrace and poverty upon him. It took years before strong drink had the entire control of him, and now it would take years to break the longing desire.

Whether his resolutions will be adequate to restrain his appetite, time alone will tell. in the meantime Smith adhered to his determination with constancy and courage.

The winter so far had been clear from ice. David was industriously employed knitting salmon and herring nets, to form a seine with a pound when they were set. Sitting by the window in his cabin one cold, raw day at work on his nets, he saw through the opening in the clump of dwarf trees, a boat with three men apparently trying to land on Mr. Lane's island. With his spy glass he recognized them as his neighbors. The boat was heading for the island, but was making use of an angle of ninety degrees for a course to get there. They were in imminent danger of being blown to sea. David without loss of time started in his wherry. But luckily their boat grounded on a rock. They managed to get out on the rock, and had passed out the jug, when the boat, relieved of their weight, floated away, and was drifting seaward with a strong north-east wind. They floundered to the shore with their boots full of water. The weather was icy cold, and it was almost night. They could just stiver* and go, having lost all except what they stood in and the jug. In this condition they arrived at the house where they were received by Smith. They handed Smith the jug and said, "Take a hearty draught; it is good for all complaints

---

*Stiver, a local word used by the fishermen.

of long standing. Smith shook his head. But they pressed him with arguments, and at last persuaded the poor fellow, whose appetite was so strong that he was about to give way, when David put in his appearance with a semblance of an accident on his part, and broke the jug. This brought a drunken howl from the men that ought to have put to shame a hyena. Their mirthful gabble now turned into frowns with deplorable complaints for the loss of the jug.

David left for home having no fear that harm or danger would come to Smith now. With a shake down of hay on the kitchen floor, Smith made them as comfortable as his circumstances would admit. When the effect of the liquor began to pass away they suffered excruciating pains with their frost-bitten feet. With many a resolution formed, and many a curse expressed, they vowed that they would never more drink liquor. Their firm resolves they kept for a time, but their ungovernable love for rum proved stronger than their vows. It was some days before they were able to go home, (two of them were always lame afterwards, but rheumatism had to bear the blame while rum went scot free.)

David's cabin seemed what it really was, the most secluded and quiet place in christendom. His favorite seat was a rustic chair ingeniously wrought by his own hands. He usually sat by the cabin window where a glimpse of the Penobscot bay could be seen through a bowery avenue, thinking of many things past, but always returning to the thought that kept his brain active—Mary.

He made no inquiry, sought for no information, and did not know what had become of her, nor would he allow any derogatory remarks about her to be made in his presence. He was logical, and tried his best not to blame her, mentally exaggerating her many virtues.

CHAPTER XVII

MARY was married, and the honey month was only too quickly gone. Her husband now must keep the pot boiling, and necessity obliged him to go to sea. Mary's home was with her husband's father who had a large family. He was good natured but inclined to be shiftless, and put off what might be done today till some other time. A farmer and a fisherman, yet neither one nor the other only when want made it absolutely necessary. Her mother-in-law was as good a woman as ever lived, but had become discouraged years ago, and had learned the bitter lesson by experience, "that what can't be cured must be endured."

Mary was a descendent from stock that would make old shears cut, and now went to work to renovate the house from cellar to garret, turning things upside down generally. She began to scrub and thump, with the soap suds flying half mast high, and drove the old man into the pig pen or some where else to smoke his pipe. The old trash that had lumbered the house for half a century was hove out of doors, or out of the chamber window helter skelter, The old cat with her kittens, her back and tail up, ran under the barn, while the yellow dog, with his tail between his legs, had taken for the woods, howling, accidently or on purpose, got scalt.

The young ones got Indian bread and milk for breakfast, dinner and supper, while the old man was served with a hakes tail and baked potatoes. It was blue Monday every day until the house was as clean as soap and sand could make it. The old man, ill at ease, thought of the hand-writing on the wall and cried, " Mene, Mene, Tekel, Upharsin."

Mary finished her scrubbing, and had the seven by nine glass replaced in the window sashes in lieu of old hats and rags. The smoky ceiling was white-washed, and the dingy walls neatly papered. The little furniture they had, Mary arranged with formal order to appear to the best advantage.

The old lady, Mary's mother-in-law, was pleased to see the old house once more neat and orderly yet sadly meditated upon the cares and troubles she had sustained. She had become weary in well doing, and remembered the time when she came to the same house a blushing bride more than a score and ten years ago with flattering hopes which were never realized.

The ways of Mary brought home to her mind her own experience. She had seen her beauty fade, fruition end in care and trouble, and hope delayed until the heart ached. Her emulation and ambition were gone.

Mary had kept her father-in-law usefully employed in cutting wood and bringing water from the spring until it was dry, which, he solemnly affirmed, had not been the case before for, fifty years. Mary with gentle entreaty persuaded the old man to clear up the external surroundings of the house, lending a hand herself when not employed alleviating her mother-in-law from the labor of the housework, which was caused in a measure by the inconveniences she was obliged to submit to, proceeding from the habit of idleness, sloth and laziness on the part of her husband, who more than thirty years ago had promised in the presence of a venerable God-fearing man that as long as his life should last he would foster and treat her with affection and support her to the best of his ability.

The old dog Jowler, a pet and favorite of the family had come home and taken up his quarters in the barn, but could not be coaxed to come into the house. A scalt dog as well as a burnt child dreads the fire. Jowler resented the ill turn and surly treatment, and Mary had one enemy in her new home, but that was a minor trouble, since she erroneously believed that dogs and fleas were inseparable.

The order of things with Mary's management of domestic affairs, stimulated the old man to a more vigorous exertion. He was hale and hearty, and some how he was ill at ease sitting in the chimney corner smoking his pipe as had been his custom, and now went to work. Only a month had passed since Mary's husband went away. In that time a great mutation had taken place, brought about by Mary's inborn peculiar bent of mind.

The weekly mail at last brought a letter for Mary from her husband. The contents informed her that he had shipped first officer of a brig bound for the island of Cuba to load sugar for a port north of Hatteras. If all went well he was in hopes to be at home in three months. Many expressions of endearment and the formal good bye, were the purport of the last letter he probably ever wrote. The brig was capsized at sea outward bound and he was drowned, and months elapsed before the sad tidings reached home.

Mary, after reading her letter until she knew it by heart, said to herself, a poor girl has got more courage than sense to marry a roving sailor. She supposed that she was now in her future home, and was zealously endeavoring to make it as comfortable as possible. Things seemed to prosper; and with fore-thought, economical management, and industry on Mary's part, brought about strange results. With her frugality she had been able to purchase an additional cow, and now had three pigs in the pen to keep the solitary pig company that had a prior right.

By hook or crook she managed to get the old man to plant an acre of potatoes in the place of the small patch which had been his usual custom. Mary and her mother-in-law worked together in harmony, and even her father-in-law liked her, notwithstanding she wheedled and coaxed him with soft words, and made him earn his bread by the sweat of his brow. Mary like all of us, was falible, and sometimes the chimney smoked; a smoky chimney is * * * * * * two bad things.

The time went on, the rose of beauty bloomed, the little tit-mouse with its shrill and wild notes sings on the branches of the aromatic Balm of Gilead tree that grows before the door. The swallows build their nests in the eaves and there rear their young. The red breasted robin skips over the green lawn with his sharp eye on the lookout.

Now here, now there, when the sweet melody of his song is heard, the husbandman makes ready for rain. In the sylvan glen while the morning sun still shades the valley, and when the cuckoo's note of love to his mate is heard, a sultry day follows.

Mary's favorite seat was on the stoop, that led to the front door with a rustic seat. Here could be seen a wild fascinating scenery diversified by woods, mountains, rugged hills and ledges,—a frequented thoroughfare where fishing and coasting vessels were continually passing. From this retreat the view facing the east was unobstructed. On the left there stood stately trees of lofty grandeur. On the right the landscape is one of undulating pastures interspersed with evergreen shrubbery, when the sable shades of night overshadow the house. Silence pervades the place, save when the sweet songs of the nightingale or the placid notes of the whippowill are heard.

The fleeting days of spring glided quickly away, like a river whose onward flowing to the ocean is rapid and free. Mary's ignorance is bliss, 'tis folly to be wise. The trite maxim told by the Sage's " Lang Syne" would be applicable now to Mary's case. She was elated, with florid hopes, fluttering with joy as she went about her work. Lark like, singing snatches of songs with her rugged health and rosy dimpled cheeks, busy as a bee, with her nimble fingers making, fixing and altering

MARY SEATED ON THE STOOP AT HER COTTAGE DOOR.

things generally and wondering what her husband would say when he came home.

The fugitive spring refuses to stay, and summer comes ushered in with gentle breezes, wafted from the Balm of Gilead tree, blended with the perfume of lavender, that grows profusely around the house. The sweet vernal grass that imparts its pleasant odor, Mary gathered in clusters and put it in the antiquated English pitchers that were common in those days in the fishermen's and sailors' cottages.

On a beautiful day in late summer, Mary was sitting on the rustic seat on the front door stoop (her usual practice) shaded by the branches of the Balm of Gilead tree. A mild west wind was blowing and a field of golden barley waving in the wind, ripe for the garner. The field in front of the house was a gradual descent to the shingle beach, a hundred rods away, washed by the tide waters of the beautiful Penobscot. Fishing boats and coasting schooners were sailing by with all their sails set and drawing. The field was shorn of its flowery verdure by the hay-makers, but yet remained a picture of beauty.

For days, weeks and months, Mary was anxiously waiting for her husband, who would never come. When the weekly mail arrived, she invariably went to the post office, rain or shine, as long as circumstances would admit, only to return disappointed.

Eight months had gone by since Mary's husband went to sea, she was now disheartened and depressed in mind and spirits. Through the long pleasant summer days she would sit on the bowery stoop thonghtfully reflecting on the past and speculating on the future. Sometimes a transient hope of possibility that her husband was living only to be rejected as a preposterous conclusion. A neighbor brought her a letter at last with a line of black on the margin of the wrapper. She startled and trembled with intuitive perceptions. It told her the sad story without breaking the seal.

Mary was chaste as a maiden, faithful when a wife, and now a widow, and more than that, all in a year.

Mary passed a lonesome winter with the old folks—she and her mother-in-law living together in unity, consoling and comforting each other in their mutual afflictions. Amidst their distress the black cloud that hung over the old homestead had a silver lining, as they had a bountiful supply of provisions for winter, an impressive difference between the stint and scantness that Mary's mother-in-law had been obliged to conform to for so many years. Her larder was stored with beef, pork and bacon; her pantry with butter and cheese; the cellar with vegetables and potatoes. In the chamber corn and barley, all brought about by Mary's ideas and intelligence.

On an early spring morning Mary left the old house to go home and live with her father, which grieved the old folks to the heart, to part with her. The neighbors with good will came to bid her farewell, and when she was ready to go, the family, neighbors, dog and all, walked with her to the shore where the boat was in waiting to take her away.

When the last good-bye was said with, "Good speed," they sadly and slowly went home. The old man said that Mary was better than gold, at the same time wiping his moist eyes with his hand.

CHAPTER XVIII.

DURING the winter the charm of solitude which David found so congenial, was broken now and then by Smith and an occasional visit from the Scotchman accompanied with some intimate crony, who were apt to stop until they wore their welcome out. When the Scotchman was present David kept the nets out of sight to avoid the Scotchman's gratuitous advice which David counted for naught. On one of the Scotchman's visits he remarked to David, "You did well last year with your weir, and not to be wondered at. You have got the best berth to take fish in there is in Penobscot bay." He said with undue fondness for his own opinion, "If I had your berth I would make a fortune." David said, "You may have it and welcome." The Scotchman's surprise was without bounds or limit. When he found his tongue he said, "That bodes no good. The moon is at the full, you have got the lune's*, and your wits have gone wool gathering." After sober second thought he made David an apology saying, "I always went off half cocked." He went home rejoicing at his own good fortune yet thinking that evil days had come to poor David, and his mind was certainly shattered. There is no uncertainty about it.

When David had completed his nets he followed his usual vocation with his gun and dog. When the tempestuous storms of March prevail he sat in his arm-chair before the cheerful fire with a book, but made a specialty of studying Aunt Nancy's old Bible. Sages of old as well as modern, have told that all men have a money price and "The love of money is the root of all evil." Be that as it may, the reverence that David had for the old Bible remains a doubtful maxim to those

---

*Affected by madness.

living that knew David well. As regards to the tenets of his religious creed he was silent, but evidently manifested his belief in prayer and devotion to his Creator and that interdiction surely followed them that failed to obey divine law.

It was early spring when David got the Rover ready to carry his primary and unique scheme into effect. Smith was to go with him, and they were to make their homes on board the schooner while tending the nets.

The locality where David set the nets was off the rocky points that project into the bay where there were coves, in lieu of a harbor, where the Rover could lay at anchor excepting in heavy weather.

From these headlands it was impracticable to build weirs owing to the depth of the water and the rocky bottom. When there was a fresh south-west wind the salmon follow the surf that breaks on the shore. On

NOTE. The migrating salmon make their appearance on the Maine coast in April and continue until July to assend the rivers for spawning .

such days they were taken in large quantities by David and Smith.

When there was a breeze at night these salmon were put on board the Rover and taken to Thomaston*, where they were turned over to an agent. With all possible dispatch, the owners then came back home to look after the nets which was absolutely necessary. This necessitated work without sleep, but the returns for fresh salmon were far in excess of the smoked.

The Scotchman with elated mind toiled early and late building the weir, still remaining tenacious of his own opinion, and locating the weir off a projecting point in a more exposed situation than where David had his weir the previous year.

His anticipations and anxiety overcame his prudence and discretion. He built the weir long before the migrating fish would arrive. When asked by an old weather-wise fisher-

*Now Rockland.

man the reason of building the weir so early, he said, "It is the early bird that catches the worm." The fisherman replied, "If we get the line gale your weir instead of catching worms will catch the devil."

The boat fishermen were ashore digging clams for bait. The tide served late when the old weather-wise fisherman said, "It is now the last of March and we have not had the equinoctial gale. The wind is north-east, do you mind how dismal and wailing the wind sounds among the trees, in my opinion we shall have heavy weather before morning."

As the old fisherman predicted, a terrible gale came on that night with an unusual high tide which played sad havoc with the Scotchman's weir. The succeeding morning the Scotchman was looking at the place where the weir was. Filled with anguish and great passion he exclaimed in Scotch dialect, "I maun be in the sheugh o' dule* and my weir

*I wish I was in h—ll.

in Scotland." The dejected and down-hearted appearance of the poor Scotchman was pitiful to look upon. The fishermen now in the place of laughing and ridiculing him at his ludicrous Scotch dialect as it had been their practice, expressed their sympathy by words and actions.

The material of which the weir was made was washed ashore and it was scattered along the shore above high water and out of the tide way. A consultation was held among the fishermen and the result was they agreed to turn to and rebuild the weir. They then ·said to the Scotchman, "You go to the main and get liquor enough." This proposition was heartily received by the Scotchman, who well knew where the rum was to be had without going to the main. A drunken debauch or carousal lasted until the weir was completed.

When they started to go home they were all more or less intoxicated. One of them

GREETING HER HUSBAND WITH ARMS AKIMBO.

had a shrew for a wife and there would be no
quiet in the house with her when he had been
drinking. He dreaded to go home and face
the music. Before he got to the house he
saw her standing in the cottage door with her
arms akimbo, ready to greet him.

With a vehement voice she said, "Where
have you been?" He answered, "My dear,
I have been helping Mr. Holiday build—"
She interrupted him, "Yes, helping Mr. Holiday get drunk. You are full of rum and hot
now. I wish the ship had sunk that brought
that Scotchman over. You are covered in
mud from your head to your heels." "My
dear, how could I help that working in the
mud flats?" She replied, "You could not
help getting drunk either. The next time
you come home hot I will fasten the doors,
and you can sleep in the barn. He then with
low murmuring said, "I will never sleep in
the barn but once." She caught the words
that were hardly intended for her ears and

replied with vehemency of anger, "What is the reason you won't?" "Cause I won't get drund again." She then took him by the arm with a griping press which made him cringe, and led him into the house.

An exuberant abundance of salmon in early days frequented the waters of Penobscot bay during the spring months. In the primitive nets of David and Smith they were caught in abundance. The Scotchman for this reason was envious of David's success, and openly manifested his emulous malice in the presence of the fishermen, who took offence at hearing the Scotchman deride David and said to him, "You are the most ungrateful man that ever lived. If it had not been for the instigation of David we would not have rebuilt your weir, now stop your slanderous tongue or we will get our bait somewhere else." This threat of menace stopped the ungrateful Scotchman's mouth. Some of the fishermen reported to David the magniloquent talk. David replied, "I have always thought that Mr. Holiday did not always have a due sense of benefits received." David entertained no enmity and had no enemies in return.

The mackerel had arrived in the bay. The fishermen reported they were fat and good size. The salmon had done running so David and Smith took up their nets, The fishermen now wanted David to fit the Rover for mackereling. She had excellent sailing qualities, and the success in many instances depends on the vessel getting where the fish have been discovered before others that are cruising in the near vicinity. When cruising they are incessently watching with a spy-glass. If one of the fleet succeed in raising a school, every vessel in sight within ten miles will be mindful of the fact in less than five minutes. Then every effort is made by the crew by spreading every available sail bowsed taut by willing hands as quickly as possible, then the trial of speed commences, the best helmsman takes the helm, and the sails are trimmed to an accuracy. It now becomes one of the most exciting scenes of a mackerel catcher. The first vessel generally heaves to under the lee-bow of the vessel that is taking mackerel and throws bait and often takes the school while the vessel on the weather their fish have ceased to bite and an end has come to their excitement. With slang maledictions they frequently greet the vessel that has taken their fish. Perhaps before the lee vessel takes a half dozen wash barrels some other vessel has hove to and to leeward, and got the school along side while they in turn denounce woe against the offender.

When the request was made by the fishermen to David to fit the Rover for mackereling he shook his head. He could not endure being in the company of the fishermen and be obliged to listen to their frivolous talk for two months at least. In sympathy however with their disappointment he would charter the Rover to them on a share if they would return her on or before the twentieth of September before the equinox, with Skipper Thomas in charge, who was an old and experienced fisherman who could keep the reckoning, and in whose confidence he could confide. These terms were satisfactory and now they were off for a cruise, and as jolly a set of old fish-killers as ever sailed over Neptune' dominion. In the Rover they were to roam on the ocean in search of mackerel and take their chances as to what fortune might bring.

To make a success in catching mackerel it requires activity and energy. The mackerel is a capricious fish and continuously changing its haunts. At times the fishermen will seek in vain for them; at other times they are plenty and voracious, and will often bite a red or white rag. The mackerel essentially differ. Some seasons they are fat and large, and found in great plentitude on the New England coast, while at others they are lean, small and scarce.

More than one young expert fisherman claims with undoubting assurance that they have caught sixty mackerel in a minute with two lines. If this rapid work is kept up the crew of a fisherman say fifteen hands, would catch a whole fare in less than half a day.*

The Elysian days of mackerel fishermen with their lines, jigs and beautiful sharp schooners have gone by. In their place the destructive steam seiners have nearly annihiliated the tinker mackerel that abounded in every cove, harbor and bay along the entire coast of Maine.

---

*This statement was published in the government report of fisheries, 1853.

ANCIENT FISHERMAN OF THE OLD SCHOOL.

CHAPTER XIX.

IT happened in the early days of the nine-
teenth century that a sudden appearance
of a school of fat mackerel came among the
islands in Penobscot bay and environs in
large quantities. They were scooped up with
pans and speared with pitchforks, and women
and children joined in the excitement pro-
puced by the remarkable and unusual appearance of mackerel.

The old fisherman in the corner by the fire
or on pleasant days on a rustic bench where
the view is unobstructed, nursing his infirm-
ity, now past labor, is more sensitive to
unkind words that are uttered by his children
or his children's wives than in the days of
yore, but yields to them on account of his
feebleness.

In early summer at the close of the day,

when the lightening bugs first made their appearance his sluggish blood quickens in his veins, and on the morrow he will try to get the boys to go with him to try once more to catch mackerel.

The singular dialect of the grizzley old fishermen a half a century or more which he considered so appropriate has not found its way as yet in the comprehensive dictionary. Their manners are coarse and harsh, their habits of life are without rule or order, but nevertheless their acts of kindness and hospitality are not exceeded by any and equalled by few; their opportunities are few to improve and their temptations are many to deviate from the true course, consequently they err through ignorance.

Chebacco boats, pinkies, jiggers were the names applied to their fishing crafts. Their provision which they called *grub*, when served up they defined as *smother*, (a pot pie) *duff*, (a pudding), *joe floggers*, (pancakes), *dunde-*

funk (fried pork, molasss and bread). When talking about oil clothes they say *ile skins*, their hat is *sou'wester*, their boots *stampers*, their knife is generally secured with a *lanyard*, (a short line), their fishing knives they term *throaters* and *splitters*, their aprons of leather or canvass, is called a *barvel*, their wives are invariably called *our wimen*. They will tell you how many shots are necessary on different fishing grounds. By a *shot* they mean thirty fathom.

They use a substitute for mittens which they call *nippers*, their boats are divided into compartments called *kits*, where they throw their fish. Their fish stories are without end, narrating their own experience and the traditions of their sires. They firmly believe in witches and dreams and will not enter on an undertaking on Friday. They will prove this belief by signs and omens that have come under their own observation. If occasion requires they will make use of their neighbor's fields to spread their bait nets caring nothing for the pre-emptive rights of the proprietors. If a remonstrance is made they will brow-beat in an arrogant manner any who dare to remind them of their trespass.

If you visit them in their cottages you will undoubtedly receive a hearty welcome, the best they have will be none too good for you. When sickness or trouble comes to their neighbors none are so ready or willing to aid and assist by night or day as they, without a thought of recompense. No matter how dark and stormy the night, they are willing to risk their lives and go to the main for the doctor.*

*See report on American Fisheries, 1853, Lorenzo Sabine of Mass-achusetts.

NOTE. When the United States Government wanted men to man their warships and gun boats in the Rebellion of 1861 to 1864, the Maine fishermen were ready and willing to serve in the Navy, volun-teered and passed examination and did their country service in all the grades from able seamen to commanders. These men knew nothing about the red tape of the old school navy and cared less. Many a valiant volunteer officer and man spent their boyhood on board a fish-ing boat.

CHAPTER XX

DAVID and Smith passed the summer in their respective boats, catching mackerel among the group of islands that are thickly scattered in the waters of the Penobscot.

On Saturdays they invariably went home to store their fish and pack and prepare them for shipment. Smith yet remained a tenant at will of Mr. Lane's, and still merited the honest confidence which David reposed in him.

David spent the Sabbath reading and deliberating with intellectual enjoyment, alone with his Bible. He was not like the world a willing slave to custom and fashion.

> " Slave to no sect, who takes no private road,
> And looks through nature, up to nature's God."

It happened on a pleasant Sunday afternoon as David sat on a rustic bench under the

spreading branches of a birch tree in meditation. The view from here the skillful artist
would fail to depict within the limits of a
single canvass. The famous painter of
scenery would be defective but the deserning
eye would preceive at a sweeping glance the
beautiful, perfect and complete whole—A
quiet stillness prevades. The maple trees
were changing their summer verdure to a
variety of shades of vermilion.

His agreeable musing was interrupted by a
strange schooner that came to anchor off Mr.
Lane's fish house, then landing a noisy set of
clamorous people ashore. David with his
spy glass observed the demon rum had full
sway, in the place of sense.

With an uneasy apprehension of danger for
Smith he went in the wherry after him and
brought him back to his cabin. Ten months
had gone by since Smith had drank or tasted
spirituous liquors, in the mean time the shame-
ful drunken revilers ran riot pillaging and des-

troying without hinderance. The fish hawks David had watched build their nest year after year on the tall spruce tree with a right prior to his own, the ruthful marauder's shot.

The next morning the marauding schooner got under way and undertook to go between the islands where there is a rocky bar extending from one to the other, not being acquainted they run the schooner ashore where she remained hard and fast. David and Smith were watching her when she struck. Smith said, "There! I am glad of it!" "No,' David replied, "You ought not to rejoice over any one's misfortune caused by rum." He said no more but his countenance was a token of his feelings. The schooner was ashore on large bowlder rocks and the tide was making ebb. When the tide left her she in all probabilities would heel off, and fill with water before she would right. David and Smith, with a few scantlings went to the schooner in the wherry with all possible haste, as "time and tide waits for no man." They had done nothing on board and did not know what to do. There was no time for talk. David acting without a medium or any intervention, with the scantling shored the vessel up, he then had the anchors let go on each side the throat halyards, made fast to the cables and hauled taut. By this means, David, with Smith's assistance saved the schooner.

The men on board the schooner were now sober (when not under the influence of ardent spirits were not corrupt beyond recovery) and now wanted to recompense David, who said to them, "You are welcome to our services in saving the schooner, should any of you in after life meet others in distress do to them as you would like to be done by, but your duty seems plain to me, your people restore to Mr. Lane the value of what he has lost, and do so no more.

Skipper Thomas was a man of mark among the fishermen, and as true to his trust as the magnetic needle of his compass to the north pole. At the specified time he dropped the anchor of the Rover off Mr. Lane's house and delivered her up to David with twenty barrels of mackerel.

Skipper Thomas and the boys as he styled them (the youngest amongst them were joging on to fifty) all hale and hearty, excepting now and then afflicted by rheumatism, but the never failing remedy in weal or woe was new rum sure, for they had taken it for a preventive and a cure times out of mind, and were willing to bear testimony of the good results.

Their mackerel had been sold and they · shared each man from two to three hundred dollars. They would winter now on the fat of the land. With buoyant spirits they loaded their wherries with their winter stores, and taking a jug of medicine to ward off an attack of the dread disease, each went to his respective home.

In October, David, Smith and Mr. Holiday put their fish on board the Rover for the Boston market. His island neighbors brought their produce and fish, and their wives sent their knitting work for David to sell or exchange.

After the Rover was loaded, for several days the weather was thick and rainy. The following Sunday morning the sun rose clear, a pacific, fair wind was blowing from an azure sky, yet David sat in contemplation on sacred things, and let the Rover swing to her anchors. The Scotchman remonstrated emphatically against losing so good a chance. David in answer said, "I will not violate the Sabbath. The Divine Book says that every man's works shall be made manifest."

In due time the Rover arrived in Boston. On the succeeding Sunday, David and Smith dressed in new clothes, were going together to the venerable Father Taylor's church. Smith, no longer with a down-cast, menial look, and a bloated face, as he walked by the side of David, but with the self-respect and dignity of a gentleman. The traces that mark the beastly vice of intemperance were gone.

When David and Smith were ready to sail Mr. Holiday was missing, and after waiting for two days they were reluctantly obliged to sail without him. The Scotchman was addicted to drink more or less strong liquor, and had probably fallen in bad company. The trite maxim still remains true, "Evil communications corrupt good manners." Mr. Holiday was never afterward seen or heard of by David or Smith. They returned home and hauled up the Rover in her winter quarters. Smith kept his good resolutions and still remained a tenant at will of Mr. Lane, and David spent the winter on an adjacent island.

CHAPTER XXI

IN the near vicinity of David there lived on an island, several families, and among them an exceedingly old couple, now unable to bear the burden and heat of the day. Owing to the infirmities of age they had become poor, notwithstanding their hundred acres and more of land. They had two cows that a kind neighbor took care of, and a flock of sheep, part of the wool of which was used by the old dame, and the residue was sold to pay the town rates. They had raised three sons and a daughter, all of whom were either dead or scattered in far off lands.

Alas, how great the change since he, with his bride, half a century ago came to the island, cleared the land of the stately trees, and built the primitive log cabin.

The aged couple often sat side by side on

pleasant days, upon a shaded seat where could be seen the waters of the Penobscot bay, which served to cheer their hearts by its beauty.

The grass is as green, the rose as fragrant, and the waters of the bubbling spring as clear and cold as in days of yore. The swallow, the robin and the bobolink still come after the vernal equinox, and depart with the first chilly breath of Boreas. The summers are as hot, and the winters are as cold now, as when he came a young man with his enchanting dreams of blue skies and sunny days.

He had lived the fleeting years of youth and manhood, all unconscious of his happiness, and in his advanced age realizes with sad regrets the joys that are past to return no more.

These old folks entertained an enthusiastic regard for David. The old lady had sent her knitting by him to Boston to exchange it for calico and groceries. His oft repeated visits were the greatest pleasure life had left for them. When David got back one of the first things he did was to go and deliver the proceeds of the knitting work, consisting of an abundant supply for winter use. The aged couple well knew that the knitting work would not bring a price to pay a tenth part of what he brought.

When the cheerless winter was ushered in by driving snow storms, the feeble old man was confined to his bed. The neighbors in turn kept his wife supplied with fuel, but most of the day she was alone with him. All the long weary nights she watched alone.

David intended to live in his cabin, and had made previous preparation to enjoy his solitude, but the thoughts of his neighbors, whose years of life were so far advanced, troubled him. The caring for them seemed to be a duty, but he was not obeying the dictates of his conscience. The consequence was he let the fire go out on his hearth, boarded up the

windows and loaded the wherry with provisions. Then with his dog and gun he went to
care for the aged people.

Imagination can hardly conceive, nor pen
describe the gratitude of this lonely couple,
now so near the sunset of their lives.

A sage of old has said, "There is a divinity
that shapes our ends." Mary, hearing of the
distress of her old neighbors, with whom she
had spent many happy hours in her girlhood
days, with tender hearted compassion for
their infirmities, decided to go and do what
she could for them, never having a thought
that David was there. So, thus, David and
Mary meet again and all brought about by a
similar spirit of benevolence dwelling in
each of their hearts. Here they passed the
winter

By want not shaken,
Nor by wealth allured,

doing everything in their power to add to
the comfort of the aged couple.

The dreary winter gave place to welcome

spring, the time for David to set his salmon nets; yet neither he nor Mary would leave the old couple to the care of strangers. David's humanity and benevolence exceeded his love for money, nor would he allow ambition to disturb his mind.

On a beautiful spring morning, the time that animates and exhilarates youth and manhood, encourages old age with flattering hopes, causes the trees to put forth their branches, the wild pear and cherry to bud and blossom, the mature old man passed away and entered

> That unseen celestial region,
> Which admits of no return.

On a conspicuous headland, thickly covered with deciduous and evergreen trees; projecting into a pacific harbor, where vessels pass and repass, and where it was a contingent occurrence for them to lay at anchor near the bold shore in heavy weather, the old man borne on a bier by his neighbors to his last resting place, was buried amidst the trees on the

THE FUNERAL.

brow of the hill. On this insular wild-wood bluff profusely grows around its verge the sweet eglantine and modest columbine.

David and Mary walked behind the coffin as their was no lineal descendant present.

At this very time an outward bound schooner* sailing to far distant lands was passing; and the old man's son, who fortuitously happened to be on board, saw his father's remains carried to the grave—a sad sight that he ever held in memory.

A venerable man of God* stricken in years with hoary locks, his head uncovered, carried the Bible, walking beside the procession to the grave, and there from the Holy Bible, he read the appropriate ninetieth psalm.

When a suitable time had passed after his interment, the proclamation in the old church on a neighboring island of an intended marriage between David and Mary was made; and this event was soon followed by a quiet wedding, and thus the twain at last were one.

*Captain William Veazie.   *Rev. William J. Durgin.

ADDENDUM.

After an elapse of forty years, the author again visited the sacred spot where the old couple lay at rest. The trees formed a gloomy barrier on all sides of the neglected graves; not a leaf fluttered, and deep solitude and silence pervaded the lonely place. While meditating on the past, the stillness was at length broken by the placid notes of a song bird. Thoughtfully I lingered there until the shades of evening settled on the insular bluff and then I reluctantly left the fascinating place.

www.ingramcontent.com/pod-product-compliance
Lightning Source LLC
Chambersburg PA
CBHW020507270326
41926CB00008B/774